Stevenson at Silverado

STEVENSON AT WORK ON *THE SILVERADO SQUATTERS*

Sketch by Joseph D. Strong, Silverado, June 1880. Heron Collection

Stevenson
at
Silverado

*The Life and Writing of Robert Louis Stevenson
in the Napa Valley, California, 1880.*

by

Anne Roller Issler

**1996
James Stevenson Publisher
1500 Oliver Road Suite K-109
Fairfield, California 94533
(707) 434-0210
e-mail at: jsp@jspub.com**

**in cooperation with the
NAPA COUNTY HISTORICAL SOCIETY**

Fourth Printing, 1996
Stevenson at Silverado
James Stevenson Publisher, Fairfield
in cooperation with the
Napa County Historical Society, and
dedicated to the memory of the author,
Anne Roller Issler

Third Printing (Revised), 1974
Stevenson at Silverado
Valley Publishers, Fresno
in cooperation with the
Napa County Historical Society

Second Printing (Revised), 1959
Our Mountain Hermitage
Stanford University Press

First Printing, 1939
Stevenson at Silverado
Caxton Press

Library of Congress Catalog Card Number: 74-81643

1996 International Standard Book Number: 1-885852-07-X

PREFACE

THOUGH a British author and a Scotsman to his bones, Robert Louis Stevenson belongs in a special way to the United States. The year he spent in the Far West was the decisive year of his life, both as human being and as artist. The winter in San Francisco, where he struggled with loneliness, defeat, starvation, illness, and the threat of death, changed him from boy to man, and the summer in rural California gave new impetus to his writing. He found a rich new fund of literary material. Out of this fund, then and later, he drew poems, essays, parts of short stories, settings for novels, and his wholly American book, *The Silverado Squatters*.

It was this autobiographical account of his honeymoon in a frontier community that introduced him to American readers and set his feet on the highroad to success. Published first as a serial in the *Century Magazine*, together with a highly enthusiastic editorial sketch of the author, it began his connection with the American publishers who were to bring him financial independence.

In the Silverado country, where he and his bride spent the summer of 1880, he lived beside the ruin of a mine. His home was a deserted bunkhouse that was falling to pieces. The people he met were innkeepers and storekeepers, prospectors and miners, stage drivers and muleteers, hunters and vintners. Stevenson admired the rugged strength of the New World and its people, and in particular he admired the frontier, as he himself called Mount Saint Helena. He was "wading deeper in the tide of life." As a result, his writing gained vigor and realism.

His summer at Silverado, however, never received adequate attention from his major biographers. Not one of them ever visited California. They missed altogether the local flavor of the countryside that so caught the imagination of R. L. S. Consequently, they were content to give the world a picture that was false in detail because based upon paucity of material.

The present volume is an attempt at a rounded picture of the Stevenson of Silverado. It is based upon first-hand interviews with neighbors who knew this Stevenson and the "characters" of whom he wrote. In no sense have these interviews been fictionalized. I have personally known several old-timers who remembered him; I have talked with scores who remembered the people portrayed in *The Silverado Squatters*. They gave me bits of information, description, anecdote, and conversation. They found heirlooms and photographs, maps, old histories, and letters. They talked with me by the hour, and asked me to call again. This is their book as much as mine. May it bring pleasure not only to lovers of Stevenson, but to all who are interested in California history.

ANNE ROLLER ISSLER

NAPA, CALIFORNIA

ACKNOWLEDGMENTS

FOR PERMISSION to quote currently copyrighted material, I am indebted to the following publishers and authors:

Longmans, Green & Company, New York, publishers of *This Life I've Loved*, by Isobel Field.

W. & R. Chambers, Ltd., London and Edinburgh, and the J. B. Lippincott Company, Philadelphia, publishers of Rosaline Masson's *Life of Robert Louis Stevenson*.

Sampson Low, Marston & Company, London, and Little, Brown & Company, Boston, publishers of *Robert Louis Stevenson, Man and Writer*, by John A. Steuart.

Doubleday, Doran & Company, New York, publishers of *R. L. Stevenson, A Critical Study*, by Frank Swinnerton.

Charles Scribner's Sons, New York, American publishers of Stevenson's own works and of his letters as edited by Sir Sidney Colvin.

I am indebted also to Mr. I. C. Adams of Calistoga, California, and the late Mr. Harry Patten, for the use of certain copyrighted photographs.

For the use of valuable collectors' items—pictures, maps, manuscripts, letters, and other Stevensoniana—I wish to thank Mrs. William Barr, San Francisco; Mrs. John E. Beck, Berkeley; Mr. Donald Crawford, Napa; Mr. Flodden H. Heron, San Francisco; and Mrs. Ethel Osbourne, Gilroy, California.

Several people shared with me their personal recollections of Robert Louis Stevenson, among them Mrs. Thomas Brown (Valentine Roch), Sonoma; Mr. Charles Crouch, Calistoga; Mr. Charles Lawley, Mount Saint Helena; Mr. William Spiers, Calistoga; Mrs. Gertrude Stratton, Oakland; Mrs. Maggie Turner, Calistoga. Although some are no longer living, I wish to list the names of all who knew Stevenson personally and contributed to this book.

Most of the older residents of Napa County knew the people in *The Silverado Squatters*. I am indebted to so many of them that this acknowledgment would read like a census report should I attempt to name them all. Those who aided me most extensively are mentioned in text or bibliography.

For the loan of books, magazines, and newspapers, my hearty

thanks to librarians and their aides at the Bancroft Library and the general library of the University of California, Berkeley; the library of Stanford University; the State Library at Sacramento; and the several libraries of Napa County. For research aid in other directions, I am grateful to the Society of California Pioneers, the California Historical Association, the Napa County Historical Society, the California State Bureau of Mines, the California State Park Commission, the Napa County recorder.

Last but by no means least, I wish to acknowledge my debt to Mr. J. H. Gipson, president of the Caxton Printers, Ltd., of Caldwell, Idaho. This book is based upon a previous volume, *Stevenson at Silverado*, published by the Caxton Printers in 1939. Mr. Gipson has not only permitted transferral of copyright, but has generously loaned several photographs from the original version of this Silverado story.

CHAPTER QUOTATIONS

Robert Louis Stevenson is quoted at the beginning of each chapter. These quotations are all from *The Silverado Squatters*, with the exception of the lines introducing "The Wedding Journey," which are from *A Modern Cosmopolis*; "Romantic Calistoga," from a "Letter to Sidney Colvin," Calistoga, May 1880; "The Hot Springs Hotel," from *Across the Plains*; "Backwoods Neighbors," from *The Amateur Emigrant*; "Literary Work at Silverado," from the "Celestial Surgeon," *Underwoods*, Book I, xxii; and "Hail and Farewell," from "In Memoriam, F. A. S.," *Underwoods*, Book I, xxvii, stanza 2.

viii

CONTENTS

ILLUSTRATIONS

Stevenson at Silverado

ROBERT LOUIS STEVENSON

Portrait in oil hitherto unpublished. By William Barr, San Francisco

The Wedding Journey

---

*Here, indeed, all is new, nature as well as
towns. The very hills of California
have an unfinished look; the
rains and streams have not
yet carved them to their
perfect shape.*

THE WEDDING had been on Wednesday, and this was
Saturday afternoon, May 22, 1880. Robert Louis Stevenson and his bride were bound for the Hot Springs at
Calistoga, a small town now less than fifty miles away,
at the head of the Napa Valley. From the window, as
their train ground to a stop, they could see a ferry slip
jutting out into the muddy water directly ahead. This,
then, was Vallejo Junction on the Carquinez Straits.
They clambered down the car steps. Another wait. What
a complicated journey! They had left San Francisco at
four o'clock, crossed the Bay by ferry, taken rail at the
Oakland pier, and for an hour or more followed the eastern shore line of San Francisco's "inland sea." Now they
must again cross that sea, here no wider than a river; and
at the South Vallejo pier again change trains—but not
until nine o'clock on the following morning. Meanwhile
they still did not know where they would spend the night.

While their train waited at the juncture point, the
bridegroom reached into the pocket of his much-worn
ulster. Always he carried with him a small notebook and

a pencil. "Bald shores and a low bald islet"—not a bad little miniature, that. Now for the great silver fog cloud "pouring in from seaward, over the hilltops of Marin County." And presently, when he could investigate at close range, he must add to his picture what looked like a tall building on the opposite shore.

As he wrote he watched the progress of the ferry that was to transport his train across the Narrows. An odd-looking ferry it was, a reconverted steamer. There was a single track down its middle that made the lower deck appear as though cut in two. Across the bow, as the strange craft drew near, he could read the name *Julia*.

His wife had gone ahead to the baggage car to get their dog. Chuchu, "a setter crossed with spaniel," was a great, soft-hearted creature, much given to laps and sofa cushions. At the San Francisco Ferry Building there had been a distressing controversy over his transportation, for which no provision had been made. Before he could so much as ride in the baggage car, Fanny must "corrupt the heart of the baggagemaster." This had not been too difficult, for Fanny, who could be aggressive and domineering, could also play the helpless lady. She knew exactly how to begin and end a harmless little flirtation, appealing to the gallant male. Before they had begun the journey, she and Louis had discussed just how they would handle emergencies en route. If a man was to be influenced, the task was hers, whereas if difficulties arose involving a woman, Louis would do the influencing. She had "softened" the baggagemaster, and now—unaccompanied, of course, by the gaunt, sallow, long-legged invalid who was her husband—she must thank him prettily while receiving Chuchu once more into her custody.

When she returned, all was in readiness aboard the ferry. And now they were off, bound for South Vallejo. Louis was still busy with his notebook. How should he describe the dreary little town that loomed ahead? "A

4

blunder," he wrote. The place was still young by the scale of Europe, but already half-deserted, like other California towns he had seen. A long pier came into view, and beyond it a wooden railway station beside the tracks. He could now see that the tall building he had observed from across the water was the Star Flour Mill. Sea-going ships lay close alongside, apparently waiting for cargoes of flour. Near by were a number of saloons, and some little distance from the shore, surrounded by marshes, was "a hotel of a great size." This, they were told, was the Frisbie House—or should he spell it Frisby?

When the ferry docked, bridegroom, bride, and dog set off in the direction of the hostelry, a two-story frame structure that had once been painted yellow. Over the hill in the distance, they had a glimpse of North Vallejo, "very white and spick and span" by contrast with the foreground. Louis felt hopeful of finding comfortable quarters at the Frisbie House, until he was near enough to see that the place was a vast ruin. Flood or earthquake had dislocated one corner of the building, "so that it hung two ways, with a great crack widest at the roof and narrowing down till it was hid by the verandah." Fanny, who had been gloomy from the start, nodded an "I told you so."

They entered by way of the bar, and the barkeeper led the way upstairs to a sort of reception room where they were to await the housekeeper. They had to huddle into the farthest corner of this most unusual room, for the house was "all fallen away toward the outside, like a piece of over-cliff." Finally a bright old lady appeared, hobbling along on a cane, and after a hearty welcome, she showed them to their bedroom.

Outside, the weather was chill and foggy. The room was cold, so they lit a fire in their stove—but got only smoke for their pains. There were two windows, with a view of dark houses and a bit of the sea, but one window wouldn't open and the other wouldn't close. There was a deafening chorus from the frogs that inhabited the marshes. Thoroughly disheartened, the bride and groom closed the bedroom door behind them and went down to dinner.

Fanny had predicted the entire bill of fare, and her predictions proved correct, right down to the dessert. It was an indifferent meal, but the little bride was hungry and ate with a hearty appetite, reserving her criticism of the cooking until later. Louis dawdled. He was more interested in further descriptions for his notebook than he was in food. The dining room reminded him of certain two-bit restaurants of San Francisco where he had dined when down on his luck. He made note of the red-and-white-checked tablecloths, the wire "hencoops" over the dishes to protect them from flies, the rough boarders eating in silence and—for a last indignity—without their coats.

When the pair emerged from the dining room, they were confronted with an emergency beside which their previous troubles shrank into oblivion. At the pier, Louis had given their baggage checks to a boy from the hotel who was to transport their several bundles and valises. It now appeared that this irresponsible creature had gone off to a lodge meeting, with the forgotten baggage checks in his pocket. But when Louis appealed for help, not only the loungers in the bar, but the clerk at the desk, merely smiled at the lad's escapade. It was an example of what might be expected of the young, they said. Whereupon Louis, deeply resenting their levity, withdrew from their presence, joined his wife outside the door, and poured forth his wrath to her.

Fanny's response was so violent that Louis soon found himself obliged to calm her down. "I breathed death on all the Frisbians," he later wrote, "but it was only she who meant it. So when the landlady appeared, a poor sick creature, to offer her apologies and the loan of night clothes, the night clothes but not the apologies were accepted by my better half. 'That is not the way to manage an hotel,' said Fanny. Whereupon the landlady, though a free-born American, actually made a sort of curtsy, and sniffed herself from the room in a very appalling temper. F., upon my representations, became so much softened that nothing would please her but to follow the landlady and apologise. It is these sudden excesses upon either hand that lead a married man to suppose himself very judicial in temper. I conceived that F. was right upon the facts; therefore, no apology; that she had been wrong in manner, therefore some sop to the landlady's feeling."

It was Louis, however, who administered the sop. He argued that if it took Fanny's feminine wiles to soften not only the baggagemaster on the train, but now also a "male understrapper" at the hotel, in order to secure care for Chuchu, then, according to the logic of their prearranged plan, the present case called for "a man to work a woman." He touched the already repentant landlady's heart with a long story about his recent illness, which melted her altogether and produced a whole armful of flannel night clothing.

Before six the next morning, husband and wife were awakened by an opera singer. What next! This hotel was full of surprises. The strong, "declamatory" voice changed from one air to another all the time they dressed, but the man's whereabouts remained a mystery.

It was too early for breakfast; only the saloons were open for business. A Sunday morning stroll was in order. Louis and Fanny "mounted the hill on a wooden footway," a kind of staircase above the marshes. The little houses that had appeared so cheerless last night in the dark now draped themselves in white roses. Mount Tamalpais, sentry to the Golden Gate, rose up in the dis-

7

tance, reminding them that even now "seamen far out at sea were scanning it with shaded eyes." And then one of the sea-going ships blossomed white with canvas, ready to sail for Liverpool with the stuff that would be English bread.

A pretty picture, but what about bread for our bride and groom? Nowhere was there any sign of breakfast. "Just then a boy came by with a milk can. Him we followed, and just about the same time a number of girls in summer dresses and each with a little book in her hand, began to appear and dot the grassy streets on their way to early Mass or some other religious exercise. From one of these we learned where milk was to be had, and found a peaceful Irishman milking a cow upon the sidewalk. His wife brought us out a bowl of new milk, which we drank leaning against the rail of the garden, and the woman standing by and looking on with kindly looks. Finally identifying us for the helpless, lost sheep couple that we truly were, she offered us coffee, took us into her poor little house and regaled us with coffee and bread and butter, to the speechless astonishment of a little, brawny, big-fisted girl child, who stared unwinkingly on Fanny from first to last, now drawing near, now backing away, but not from terror, merely, as it seemed to change the point of view."

The hospitable Irishwoman, who doubtless reminded him of Mary Carson, his San Francisco landlady, would not accept Louis Stevenson's coin in pay, so he gave it to the child "to buy candy with," thinking perhaps of another child, little Robbie Carson, now happily recovered from the pneumonia through which Louis had helped to nurse him before falling ill on his own account. Well, the grim winter was past and done. After years of waiting, he and Fanny were man and wife. They were embarked upon springtime adventures. Before the summer was over, he would meet other people as plain and good as his

South Vallejo hostess; though he did not know it, he would live in another house as ruinous as Frisbie's hotel; and assuredly he would fill many pages of his notebook with description and incident.

One more page he must record before boarding the train this Sunday morning for Calistoga. "When we got back to the neighborhood of the Frisby House, the strong, tottering voice of the singer was still the only living sound. His spirits seemed to have brightened as the morning advanced; for now he launched himself into florid arias, with many a run and tremolo; perhaps it was from the age, I might almost say the antiquity, of his voice, but there seemed a dash of something false in the high spirits of the performance; a sad heart perhaps in this morning chanticleer. We learned he was once an opera singer, and now occupied a little shop in that yellow ruin of a Frisby House, where he cobbled old clothes at a dollar the job. Every morning, at the same unseasonable hour, he was to be heard a-chanticleering with that old voice over his repairs; what time the frogs left off, he struck up; so that neighborhood of marshes and saloons was never long without music of a sort. It seems that some one had hurried down that morning to warn him that there were strangers whom he might disturb; and he had promised cheerily 'to *try* to sing a little lower.' I liked that word; and I was still more pleased to think that, if he tried, he had failed so signally."

The kindly R. L. S., at the end of his page, concluded that we are all poets and singers at heart, "though the verses of some of us, and the songs of others, are better reserved strictly for ourselves and God."

Before nine o'clock the lost baggage had been found and rechecked, the hotel bill had been paid, and the lap-loving Chuchu was again entrained after his mistress had accomplished the softening of another baggage-man's heart. Louis and Fanny took their places in the single day coach, along with a few other passengers, and the Sunday morning train of the Napa Valley Railroad pulled out for Calistoga.

"For some way beyond Vallejo the railway led us through bald green pastures. On the west the rough highlands of Marin shut off the ocean; in the midst, in long, straggling, gleaming arms, the bay died out among the grass; there were few trees and few enclosures, the sun shone wide over open uplands, the displumed hills stood clear against the sky. But by-and-by these hills began to draw nearer on either hand, and first thicket and then wood began to clothe their sides; and soon we were away from all signs of the sea's neighborhood, mounting an inland, irrigated valley. A great variety of oaks stood, now severally, now in a becoming grove, among the fields and vineyards. The towns were compact, in about equal proportions, of bright new wooden houses and great and growing forest trees; and the chapel bell on the engine sounded most festally that sunny Sunday, as we drew up at one green town after another, with the townsfolk trooping in their Sunday's best to see the strangers, with the sun sparkling on the clean houses, and great domes of foliage humming overhead in the breeze."

At Napa, the county seat, the train halted for some time, giving the scribbler in the day coach an opportunity to admire the Palace Hotel, an imposing building that stood opposite the new-looking railway station. Beyond, as the engine chugged forward, he caught a glimpse of the Embarcadero de Napa, where a sailing ship and a steamer were tied up after unloading cargo. What luck that travelers no longer had to change at the Napa wharf from a wheezy two-wheeler to a rocking stagé coach! One could balance one's notebook on window sill or lap while sketching out the descriptions that would later be expanded.

Beyond Napa the valley narrowed and the hills drew

closer together. Comfortable farmhouses with dormers and verandas followed each other along the highway that paralleled the track. Beyond the flower gardens that surrounded them were orchards and vineyards. This was *green* country, watered by natural streams. It was a country differing from the "rich and varied" Middle West, which the scribbler had enjoyed; differing still more from the gray-brown desert of Wyoming, Utah, and Nevada, which he had not enjoyed at all. He thought the Napa Valley was like southern France, where he felt most happy and at home.

Now came Yountville, Oakville, Rutherford, Bello, Saint Helena, Barro, Bale, and Walnut Grove, most of them mere stops along the railway. Their American place names were as odd and interesting as any the scribbler had encountered on his trip across the plains. Saint Helena, a sizable town, was a gem among the vineyards. He must return to investigate her wines.

The mountain ranges that bordered the valley grew ever higher, steeper, and more jagged. Years later, Louis Stevenson told a San Francisco newspaperman that in their rugged beauty they reminded him of the Swiss Alps. One crag looked like a great cathedral perched high up on the path toward heaven. Now the mountain ranges drew together to form the apex of a triangle, and, standing forth ever clearer until she filled the sky, Mount Saint Helena reared her dark dome. The train, a few minutes before noon, came to a final halt at the Calistoga railroad station. A short time later, bride and groom had registered at the Hot Springs Hotel, where they awaited the call to dinner.

Romantic Calistoga

-------◆◆◆►-------

*Here we are, Fanny and I, and a certain
hound, in a lovely valley under Mount
Saint Helena, looking around, or
rather wondering when we
shall begin to look
around, for a house
of our own.*

No ONE who saw his signature—the desk clerk at the
Springs Hotel, the postmaster, the local editor, the storekeeper—thought it a matter for excitement that Robert
Louis Stevenson was in Calistoga. His name had no
news value. To the people who occupied Calistoga's
small frame cottages in that summer of 1880, a certain
loiterer in their midst—a tall man of thirty, stooped,
sallow, very thin—was merely a summer stranger, one
of the hundreds of health seekers who came yearly to the
Hot Springs. "He didn't mix much," they later explained. Instead, he was often seen scribbling in the notebook he kept in his pocket.

The stranger was vastly more interested in the town
than the town was interested in him. Already he was at
work on a tale that would immortalize the place and its
people. He had written an English friend about the notes
he was keeping. "I think my new book should be good:
It will contain our adventures for the summer, in so far

as these are worth narration; and I have already a few pages of diary which should make up bright."

These first pages concerned his trip from San Francisco with his bride and their overnight stop at the oddly wrecked hotel in South Vallejo. Other pages had been added. Since his arrival in Calistoga he had written several little sketches concerning Mount Saint Helena, for the mountain fascinated him. Once he wrote, "And there was something satisfactory in the sight of that great mountain that enclosed us to the north: whether it stood, robed in sunshine, quaking to its topmost pinnacle with the heat and brightness of the day; or whether it set itself to weaving vapours, wisp after wisp growing, trembling, fleeting, and fading in the blue."

There were nice little bits about the town, too. He wrote a description of the main street that was to remain accurate for generations to come. Details would change, buildings would burn down and be replaced, but in general outline those four blocks between the depot and the highway would remain as he described them.

"The railroad and the highway come up the valley about parallel to one another. The street of Calistoga joins them, perpendicular to both—a wide street, with bright, clean, low houses, here and there a veranda over the sidewalk, here and there a horse-post, here and there lounging townsfolk. Other streets are marked out, and most likely named; for these towns in the New World begin with a firm resolve to grow larger, Washington and Broadway, and then First and Second, and so forth, being boldly plotted out as soon as the community indulges in a plan. But, in the meanwhile, all the life and most of the houses of Calistoga are concentrated upon that street between the railway station and the road. I never heard it called by any name, but I will hazard a guess that it is either Washington or Broadway. Here are the blacksmith's, the chemist's, the general merchant's, and Kong

Sam Kee, the Chinese laundryman's; here, probably, is the office of the local paper (for the place has a paper—they all have papers); and here certainly is one of the hotels, Cheeseborough's, whence the daring Foss, a man dear to legend, starts his horses for the Geysers."

An old map of 1871 indicated that the residential section, then as later, extended but a few blocks north, south, and west, being cut short on the east by foothills. The Napa River wound its sinuous way through the town, which claimed five hundred residents. The newest resident apparently never saw this map, dearly as he loved all maps, for the name of Calistoga high street was clearly printed out; it was neither Washington nor Broadway, but Lincoln Avenue.

The daring Foss had a page to himself in the notebook, for this was the man with whom Stevenson held his first telephone conversation.

"California boasts her famous stage-drivers, and among the famous, Foss is not forgotten. Along the unfenced, abominable mountain roads, he launches his team with small regard to human life or the doctrine of probabilities . . . . I only saw Foss once, though, strange as it may seem, I have twice talked with him. He lives out of Calistoga, at a ranche called Fossville. One evening, after he was long gone home, I dropped into Cheeseborough's, and was asked if I should like to speak with Mr. Foss. Supposing that the interview was impossible, and that I was merely called upon to subscribe the general sentiment, I boldly answered 'Yes.' Next moment, I had one instrument at my ear, another at my mouth, and found myself, with nothing in the world to say, conversing with a man several miles off among desolate hills. Foss rapidly and somewhat plaintively brought the conversation to an end; and he returned to his night's grog at Fossville, while I strolled forth again on Calistoga high street."

MOUNT SAINT HELENA FROM CALISTOGA

Photograph by I. C. Adams

"This pleasant Napa Valley is, at its north end, blockaded by our mountain." —R. L. S. in *The Silverado Squatters.*

LINCOLN AVENUE, CALISTOGA, AS IT WAS IN STEVENSON'S DAY

Courtesy Wm. Spiers

"The railroad and the highway came up the valley about parallel to one another. The street of Calistoga joins them, perpendicular to both—a wide street, with bright, clean, low houses, here and there a veranda over the sidewalk, here and there a horse-post, here and there lounging townsfolk."—R. L. S. in *The Silverado Squatters.*

Colonel Clark Foss had installed his one-man line during the previous year, and interest was still running high. The *Independent Calistogian* reported that "telephones are now in use on the telegraph line between Calistoga, Fossville, and Kellogg. They are found to be a great convenience." Even San Francisco had been without telephones until 1876, and only the great hotels and the most important business houses could boast them in 1880. Never during his months in Monterey, San Francisco, or Oakland had Stevenson had occasion to test the miraculous contraption. And now behold, in this frontier village, "running far ahead among the Indians and the grizzly bears," here was a telephone and he had spoken into the mouthpiece and heard another man's voice in reply.

The famous stage driver's starting point at the Calistoga end of the route was the Magnolia Hotel, property of Jack Chesebro, a Yankee forty-niner. In all probability the original spelling of the name was the one Stevenson gave it, Cheeseborough; but Jack didn't spell it that way, or at any rate it did not so appear in local histories. Amusingly enough, R. L. S. was·as easily incensed as most people when his own name was misspelled, yet he was notoriously negligent of the names of others. He misspelled all but one or two of the names of the people he put into *The Silverado Squatters*, though not enough to disguise them, if that was his purpose.

Jack Chesebro was the hero of a real-life adventure story. He had gone to sea in his youth and sailed around the Horn to California in the clipper ship, *Contest*. He'd tried mining in Sierra County and amassed enough gold to become the proprietor of the Revere House at Napa. Coming to Calistoga twenty years later as an employee of Sam Brannan, he had in 1876 built the Magnolia Hotel, directly across the street from the Calistoga post office and telegraph office on Lincoln Avenue. The Magnolia was an imposing structure for a frontier village, with forty bedrooms and several bathrooms. The latter were supplied with "warm water and cool water for the tub and shower, and also with Hot Sulphur Water from a hot sulphur well on the premises."

The keeper of this hotel was not the only adventurer whose life story interested Robert Louis Stevenson that summer. At Monterey he had known a frontiersman "who was out with the bear flag and under Fremont when California was taken by the States." In and about Calistoga were a dozen such frontiersmen, for this region had furnished most of the rebels who marched on Sonoma, took General Mariano Vallejo prisoner, and raised the bear flag. Several were still living. They never tired of telling their story of the California Republic.

Still living also were several of the *californios* who had preceded them. Loyal subjects of Mexico, these had received land grants of thousands of acres, ranchos now beset with squatter troubles. On his Sunday morning trip up the valley, Stevenson had seen two of their old adobe houses—a small one, the earliest adobe in the valley, built by Cayetano Juarez at the southern extremity of Napa; and a more palatial one, built by Salvador Vallejo at the northern extremity. Don Salvador, brother to the Sonoma general, had died four years before, but Don Cayetano, despite his almost fourscore years, could still relate the history of his Tulocay grant, which, when he'd received it in 1841, had been one vast pasture of wild oats for his herds of horses and cattle.

In the upper part of the valley, where Calistoga now stood, most of the families bore the names of early Americans. Their forebears had crossed the plains with the first of the emigrant trains. The grandfathers and grandmothers liked very well to tell of their experiences en route to California, of the little American farms they had founded on land bought or earned from the Mexicans, of the grizzlies and other wild animals who had molested their hogs and sheep. Nor were all their stories grim. They had pleasant memories of community house raisings and chinking bees, of weddings and of christenings.

Stevenson was interested especially in the stories they told of the Indians. About fifty were still living in the county, a pitiful remnant of the thousands who had roamed its lush meadows and rough hills before the arrival of the white man with his firewater and firearms, his strange gods and stranger diseases. The Mayacomas, one of the six tribal groups that once inhabited the valley, had occupied the level plain at the base of Mount Saint Helena, the very spot where Stevenson was now living. The village braves had bathed in the hot wells of what they called the "oven place." Only a decade before Stevenson himself bathed there, half-naked Indians were still to be seen on the hotel grounds, mingling with guests clad in the height of fashion.

The visitor from Scotland wondered much about these Napa Valley Indians. While crossing the plains on his way to San Francisco, he had thought of that vast territory as the red man's "hereditary continent." Fair to both sides, he had visualized first the emigrants striking out for new homes in the West, then the Indians as they were pushed farther and farther back, their hunting grounds seized, their spirits broken. He marked places on the map associated with tragedy for the white man; but he saw, too, that from the Indian's point of view here was a chapter of American history "of injustice and indignity such as a man must be in some ways base ·if his heart will suffer him to pardon and forget."

He had written of Indians at Monterey, his pity going out to those few still hanging about the Mission at Carmel. He had incorporated Indian legend in his writing of San Francisco. On his journey up the Napa Valley he had visualized the land before plows had broken the sod, before sawmills had taken the largest trees. Arriving in Calistoga, he had asked questions of his neighbors. "In this district," he learned, "all had already perished: redwoods and redskins, the two noblest indigenous things, alike condemned."

The emigrants had pushed out the Indians, but they had lived their own chapter well. Thrifty, industrious, and brave, they had brought civilization and helped build a great state. The Calistoga people would have been amazed to learn how much Stevenson knew of their forebears. Ever since his arrival in New York almost a year ago, he had been reading American history. Always he must see a new place, and himself in it, against the perspective of the past. To him, Calistoga was the American West in microcosm. Here the past blended with the present. The people of the region not only interested him as worthy human beings, they stimulated him to a new writing effort. These people he must describe.

They could tell him stories handed down by their parents, stories of the "childlike" red men; of the padres seeking a site for the Mission later located at Sonoma; of the Russian explorers turning inland from Bodega to investigate the peak they named Saint Helena; of the Hudson Bay trappers bringing their squaws from the far north to be married at the Mission; of the American mountain men, George Yount and James Clyman, still living in the valley; of the Spanish-Mexican ranchos still outlined on the county maps; of the scores of American pioneers who settled here before their country possessed the state. There were survivors of the Donner Party in Calistoga who could tell him stories more terrible than he was ever to write; there were miners who had found at Coloma more gold than he was ever to earn.

The very remoteness of this backwoods country offered a challenge to his restlessly creative mind. Here

CALISTOGA CLOSE-UPS

Group of drawings by E. S. Moore

SPRING GROUNDS AND RACE TRACK

Drawing, 1865. Artist unknown

was a region such as he had never known. Here were people such as he had never described. Before he and Fanny had so much as begun their house-hunting up the side of Mount Saint Helena, he was at work, sketching in outlines, putting down phrases that would become sentences, then paragraphs, then pages. He visualized the cities, factories, railroads of a future that was never to come; "yet in the meantime," he wrote, "around the foot of that mountain the silence of nature reigns in a great measure unbroken, and the people of hill and valley go sauntering about their business as in the days before the flood."

The Silverado Squatters was taking shape.

The Hot Springs Hotel

---

*It is the settlers, after all, at whom we have
a right to marvel.*

OFTEN, as in San Francisco during the months just past, the Scot lately arrived at the Hot Springs wrote in bed. There were days when his anxious bride feared an imminent relapse. On one of these days she persuaded him to move from the main hotel building to one of the numerous cottages on the grounds, a cottage not unlike her former home in Oakland where she had been his nurse. Here he could have not only greater privacy but extra food. To supplement the meals served him in the big dining hall, Fanny ordered milk from near-by neighbors.

Stevenson's "little milkmaid," Gertrude Walker, was then a child of twelve. Many years later, after she had married Dr. Robert Thompson Stratton, she told the story of her friendship with the fascinating stranger.

"His cottage was one of six in a row, all alike. It was the first inside the entrance to the grounds, near what is now a modern bathhouse adjacent to the Calistoga airport. It was there that mother let me deliver a quart of milk each evening. Father had it brought from our farm. We were living for a few months at the Mansion House, close to the other bathhouse, where the geysers attract so many visitors.

"When I brought the milk, Mr. Stevenson would be lying on his couch, sometimes on the porch, sometimes under the palm tree. He asked me many questions and told me jokes and stories. I remember his travel stories especially. They interested me so much that I am sure they had something to do with my own later calls at 'ports and pleasant places.' We played games, especially mumblety-peg. When he was told that he must pull the peg out with his teeth, he looked shocked, but just then his wife appeared with a glass of milk and saved the situation.

"Mr. Stevenson was tall and thin, typically Scotch in build. Later, in my travels, I saw many men in Scotland who reminded me of him. His conversation with me, a child, was animated, and I, who was always a talker, enjoyed it greatly."

Not all the invalid's daytime hours were spent lying on the couch. After breakfast there was a quiet spell with his notebook, usually out of doors, then the mail to read and answer. In midmorning he and Fanny sometimes tried the hot baths. They had a wide choice—the large enclosed swimming pool, the smaller chemical baths, or the pagodas on the lawn. These last offered hot mud baths or Russian steam baths, the parboiled bather regulating the flow of fresh air by means of slides in the walls of the cabinet.

In the middle of the day it was often too hot to move about. A siesta was then in order. But when the sea breeze sprang up about four o'clock, the bride and groom ordered the horses they had brought from Oakland and went for a canter. Later they strolled about the grounds and drank of the hot water that tasted like chicken broth. They were usually alone, and they made an odd-looking pair—the gaunt young man with his longish hair, brilliant eyes, and restless hands, his bizarre and shabby clothing, his distinguished reserve of manner; and the short, thickly set, "dusky" woman, past forty, with her decisive ways, her firm chin and boyish shock of heavy hair, and her compelling eyes that could flash in anger one minute and melt in pity the next.

And an odd pair they were, indeed. The groom was a gently reared son of Scotland, descended from a long line of outstanding engineers and covenanting clergy. His had been a sickly, too-long-coddled childhood, a rebellious youth, a young manhood of diligent work at writing that early proved his genius. Never until this year in California had he lacked comparative wealth, never until now had he worried about supporting a family.

His wife's background contrasted sharply with his own. She was an American of Dutch and Swedish ancestry, almost twelve years his senior, by temperament independent and domineering, as Louis had already learned. While at the Frisbie House at South Vallejo, he'd confided to his diary an emotional scene between Fanny and the landlady that illustrated her remarkable force of character "which (occasionally) I so much admire in her." She had grown up in pioneer Indiana and spent her childhood in tomboy sports. Coming early to maturity, she had married at sixteen and lived thereafter the rude life of mining camps in a still lawless West, several times separated from her husband, mothering three children and at times supporting them.

This strangely contradictory pair had met in France four years before. Fanny had had a bitter disagreement with her husband, Sam Osbourne, who, in the words of one of their friends, was "thoroughly devoid of family instincts." With her teen-age daughter and two little boys, Fanny had gone to Paris to continue the art study begun in San Francisco, and here lost her four-year-old son under circumstances of great pathos. As a result, she suffered a "nervous crisis," with mild hallucinations and acute forgetfulness. Upon the advice of an American friend, she had gone to Grez, a French artists' colony, to regain health and spirits. The flattering attentions of the gay, brilliant young writer, Robert Louis Stevenson, had distracted her mind and won her heart. Both the youth and the woman were in rebellious mood, he against the Puritan standards of a too-strict childhood and the loss of another woman he had loved, she against an unhappy marriage and the loss of her child; and the love affair in which they presently found themselves involved was not a surprising result.

For the next two and a half years the pair had seen much of each other, Fanny continuing her studies in Grez and in Paris, Louis working steadily at writing, in France and at home in Edinburgh. Erratic, emotional, often hysterical, the young Scotsman during this time of stress went suddenly blind. Fanny cared for him in her Paris apartment until she could take him to his friends in London. Here she fell ill herself and while convalescing met many of those who had been his close companions and found them congenial. In the fall of 1878, after several postponements, she returned to the United States, with a half-formed plan to divorce her husband. And a year later Louis followed.

Fanny had gone to Monterey to recuperate from the strain and worry of their year of separation. With her were her two children, Isobel and Lloyd, and her sister Nellie, who presently contracted diphtheria. Sam Osbourne came down from Oakland week ends. He was still supporting the family; but Fanny, deep in consultation with legal friends about her divorce, feared desertion. She worked frantically at both writing and painting to earn money. Sam had rented rooms in the Bonifacio adobe on Alvarado Street. After he arrived, Louis lived for a time in another adobe across the street and later in the French Hotel. He had gone alone on a camping trip, become ill, and had been forced to return to Monterey for medical attention. He was eating one meal each day in the Bohemian Restaurant of Jules Simoneau, "sponging" the rest, or going without. Life was far from rosy for any of the three people caught in an age-old triangle—Sam Osbourne, his wife, or Louis Stevenson.[1] Here was misery, as well as joy.

In December, Fanny having returned to her husband's cottage in Oakland, Stevenson rented a cheap room in San Francisco at 608 Bush Street. He continued his fevered efforts to support himself, but with little result, and at last became so gravely ill that his doctors despaired of his life. Fanny had him moved across the Bay and doggedly nursed him back to comparative health. At about the time the divorce proceedings ended, there came an epochal cablegram from Stevenson's father promising financial help, and then came their simple wedding in San Francisco. A few days later they were on their way to the Hot Springs where they now found themselves.[2]

Oddly enough, it was Fanny's divorced husband, unstable, easy-going, but freely endowed with generosity and charm, who had arranged that the honeymoon of the just-married pair be spent at Calistoga. Throughout the divorce proceedings he had remained the courteous, affable man of the world that he was, with no trace of vengeance toward the lover who succeeded him in his wife's affections. A shorthand court reporter, he'd supported Fanny until he lost his job. In April he'd opened his home to the ailing Stevenson, quietly stepping out of the picture, and when finally the divorce was granted, he'd written a letter of introduction to "an hotelkeeper at Calistoga, a hamlet in Napa County, where the honeymoon might be spent economically."

This hotelkeeper was George W. Johnson, at that time owner of the Hot Springs, a relic of the Gold Rush and a

[1] See *No More a Stranger*, by Anne B. Fisher, Stanford University Press, 1946.

[2] *Happier for His Presence*, by Anne Roller Issler, Stanford University Press, 1949.

unique example of the strange contrasts in the social life of early California.

The tide of Americans that swept into Napa Valley with the mining excitement had spread abroad tales of boiling water, of geysers a hundred feet high. In 1859 there came a wealthy man whose purpose was to build a great watering place that would compare with the famous spas of Europe. This man was Samuel Brannan, California's arch-pioneer, the ablest of her early American settlers.

During the time that Louis and Fanny Stevenson were guests of the hotel until recently owned by him, Brannan was in Mexico. Two years before, he had established the Sonora Colonization Society, and this summer was making surveys for a railroad there.

Stevenson, in *The Silverado Squatters*, described him simply as "the man who found the springs." A great pity that writer and settler never met, for this man's exploits would have made exciting reading. One of the strangest of the strange assortment of wealth seekers who came to California with the war of 1846, he was a down-Maine Yankee turned Mormon elder. In San Francisco's Portsmouth Square, Stevenson must often have heard the story of how the company of men, women, and children Brannan brought around the Horn camped there before building their homes among the sandhills. He must have known of Brannan's San Francisco newspaper; of his San Antonio Pottery in East Oakland, not far from the Osbourne cottage; of the fortune amassed in land speculation and trade with the gold miners.

A cool half million dollars of that fortune went into the buildings and grounds of the Hot Springs Hotel. This was the man's most ambitious project; here his zest for pioneering had full sway. He induced other settlers to start taverns and stores, and rewarded their enterprise by influencing the state legislature to aid in the construction of the Napa Valley Railroad, with himself as its first treasurer. The town of Calistoga was his creation. Even the name was Brannan's. Boasting that he would make this little health resort the Saratoga of California (at a supper party, according to Stevenson), he spliced the names of California and Saratoga, and created "Cal(is)toga."

During the 'seventies there were sometimes as many as a thousand guests at the Hot Springs in a single month. And what an incongruous place to come upon in the midst of wilderness. The grounds covered two thousand acres, extending from the hillock, Mount Lincoln, to the base of Mount Saint Helena on one side and to the railroad on the other. Near Mount Saint Helena were a vineyard of a hundred acres, a Japanese tea garden, and a mulberry orchard with a cocoonery. Across the tracks was the brandy distillery owned by Brannan in partnership with Lewis Keseberg, a survivor of the Donner Party. The rambling hotel with its cluster of bathhouses was built at the foot of Mount Lincoln, whereon stood a reservoir and an observatory. To the east of the hillock was a long, low building designed by Brannan "as a sort of reform school for friendless youths of hoodlumish proclivities." To the west was a skating pavilion. Surrounding the central group of buildings were two wide, circular avenues enclosing an elaborate park of forty-four acres. Adjoining this park were another forty acres, enclosing a race track and stables. At equal distances on Wapoo Avenue, the inner circle, twenty-five little cottages faced the hotel, built for the convenience of guests who preferred the privacy of their own domicile.

These cottages were identical in room plan and general outline, differing only in the pattern of the scrollwork under the roofs of the verandas. The cottage Stevenson occupied in 1880 was at the juncture of the circle

BATHING PAVILION AND SKATING RINK, SPRING GROUNDS, CALISTOGA

Drawing. Artist unknown

SAM BRANNAN'S HOTEL, CALISTOGA IN THE BACKGROUND

Old drawing, artist unknown (about 1865)

with the thoroughfare leading to Calistoga. A little boy who lived near by often saw a tall, emaciated, foreign-looking visitor going in and out there.

"I was a boy of ten," Charley Crouch liked to tell in after years. "My father had rented one of the cottages of the circle surrounding the hotel, and for a short time Stevenson lived in another. It stood under that line of palms you can still see to the west of Mount Lincoln. I often saw Mr. Stevenson strolling about the grounds. He and Mrs. Stevenson used to ride their ponies out of the gate and go off into the country. They brought two little Canadian ponies in here, which they later sold. My father bought Stevenson's pony for me, and I had him for ten years, turning him out to pasture in 1890. Stevenson had named him Star, and he was a beautiful little saddle horse, dark brown in color. Major Johnson, who ran the hotel, bought Mrs. Stevenson's pony, Clavel, for his daughter."

In the heyday of its glory, several drawings were made of the hotel and its surroundings. They were unsigned but were probably the work of Professor J. S. Silver, a visitor at the hotel. A similar drawing, over his name, appeared in the *Calistoga Tribune*, February 27, 1873. It bore the title, "Calistoga Springs." All five pictures illustrate with exactitude Stevenson's description in *The Silverado Squatters*.

"Alone, on the other side of the railway, stands the Springs Hotel, with its attendant cottages. The floor of the valley is extremely level to the very roots of the hills; only here and there a hillock, crowned with pines, rises like the barrow of some chieftain famed in war; and right against one of these hillocks is the Springs Hotel—is or was; for since I was there the place has been destroyed by fire, and has risen again from its ashes. A lawn runs about the house, and the lawn is in its turn surrounded by a system of little five-roomed cottages,

27

each with a veranda and a weedy palm before the door. Some of the cottages are let to residents, and these are wreathed in flowers. The rest are occupied by ordinary visitors to the hotel; and a very pleasant way this is, by which you have a little country cottage of your own, without domestic burthens, and by the day or week."

From his own cottage on the western extremity of the lawn, Stevenson—always an early riser when able to be up—sometimes walked across to the main building before six o'clock in the morning. The grounds were less well cared for than in the 'seventies, the path less smooth, the grass less green; but on the other hand, the trees had grown tall to protect him from the summer sun, which sometimes sent the thermometer soaring into the nineties even at this hour of day. Scattered about the lawn were the numerous small bathing pavilions, shaped like pagodas, with whose inner workings he and Fanny had become familiar. Ahead was the cactus-crowned, pine-shaded hillock, Mount Lincoln. A century plant was blooming there this summer, and each week the *Independent Calistogian* reported its progress.

The hotel, like the grounds, had grown shabby with the years. In the days when the Licks, the Hearsts, the Stanfords mingled here with stars of the opera and the stage, the parlors had been richly furnished with soft carpets, imported furniture, priceless oil paintings. Liveried servants had waited on the guests. The service was more casual nowadays, but the place was still comfortable, and the food was excellent.

If only prices hadn't been so high. How could Osbourne have thought the Springs "economical?" Imagine cottage, meals, and mineral baths costing ten dollars per week per person! While Stevenson, shabby and a little unkempt, ordered his breakfast, he indulged in his daily worry over expenses. He had been making inquiries of the townspeople regarding living quarters that would cost next to nothing. One could find squatters' quarters in deserted mining camps hereabouts. He hoped to find a place at a high enough altitude to escape the fogs from the Pacific, which even here at the head of Napa Valley still occasionally plagued him. Maybe, when he found the place, Fanny would stop worrying about his cough.

Meanwhile he would see as much as possible of Calistoga and the surrounding country. Diligently he would record his impressions, for he must get on with his story of the summer.

Stage Drivers and Highwaymen

---

*It must be remembered that we are here
in a land of stage drivers and highwaymen; a land, in that respect,
like England a hundred
years ago.*

WATCHING the stages draw up in front of "Cheeseborough's," Stevenson remembered the coaches that rumbled
through the novels of Charles Dickens. He thought of the
mountain roads and inns of England and Scotland, roads
and inns associated with stage robbers, real or fictitious.
Here in the California mountains, by some magic akin to
Aladdin's, he had been whisked backward in time a full
century. The coaches that lined up every morning before
the Magnolia Hotel were real. The drivers were his con-
temporaries. And the bandits who harried them on the
road were a present menace to all who traveled across
Mount Saint Helena.

Most of the commercial travel through this region,
whether to towns, mining camps, or resorts, was by stage.
Resorts were especially numerous. "The whole neighborhood of Mount Saint Helena," as Stevenson had
noted, "is full of sulphur and of boiling springs," and
almost every cluster of springs was surrounded by hotel
buildings. This was the vacation season and each week
the local papers reported on travel to the White Sulphurs,
Aetna, and the numerous spas of Lake County.

30

On the less traveled roads the stage might be a two-or three-seated rig of the buggy or surrey type, but on the main lines it was most often a genuine Concord coach, with passengers both inside and on top, its "boots" filled with baggage and mail, and the express box stowed under the driver's seat for safety. The roads the drivers followed had been hacked out of the hillsides. The six or eight horses that drew the large Concords swept daringly around the numerous curves and over the rocky creek crossings, the coaches swinging dizzily on their thorough-brace leather springs.

By far the most famous driver was Clark Foss. Menefee's *Sketchbook*, earliest history of Napa County and the surrounding country, described him as world renowned and "second to none in the handling of horse, whip, and lines." And Stevenson was fascinated by the man. "Flinching travellers, who behold themselves coasting eternity at every corner, look with natural admiration at their driver's huge, impassive, fleshy countenance."

Locally known as the Old Chieftain, Foss had inherited his stage line from his father, who drove the first coach and six to the Big Geysers by way of the old road through Healdsburg in 1863. Beyond the highest point was the Hog's Back, connecting two ranges of mountains, where the traveler felt himself literally on the ridgepole of the world, with so sheer a drop on either side that the valleys were invisible. Then came the sudden tortuous descent into the Pluton Canyon and the cry, "All out!" at the Geysers Hotel. With death stalking every foot of the road, the "mouth of Hell" with its spouting geysers, its vividly colored rocks, and its subterranean roar, was a downright relief.

The younger Foss later built a less dangerous but equally scenic road. The distance by the old road was twenty-six miles and the fare was twenty-five dollars. The new Knight's Valley road cut off six miles, but whether the Old Chieftain also cut the fare local history failed to mention. His road was vividly described by a little girl who lived at the McDonald Ranch on the way to the geysers. The child, later Mrs. Maggie Turner of Calistoga, was more afraid of Foss, she said, than if he'd been a rattlesnake. "He was rough and gruff, a great big giant of a man, and the way he drove his horses was enough to make your hair stand on end. I rode behind him many a time, scared as I was. In these days there aren't mountain roads like there were then, so you can't picture what the experience was like. He'd built the road to the Big Geysers himself—an ungraded seven-foot shelf on the mountainside, unprotected by wall or fence, with drops of several thousand feet to the valleys and curves so sharp you couldn't have seen anyone coming till too late to avoid a collision, only of course his terrific yell would have warned them. More people came to ride behind the Old Chieftain than came to see the geysers, wonderful though they were."

When Foss moved to Calistoga, Maggie's father, Frank McDonald, became the host at Foss House. The hotel register, dating back to 1864, eventually came into the possession of the daughter. Numerous toasts to the driver were appended to the signatures. After the experiences of the journey, passengers stopping at Foss House seemed to spout verse as naturally as the geysers spouted steam.

> Here's to Foss, his reins and his whip,
> That gave us such a jolly trip.
>
> Of Foss himself we need say no word,
> A host in himself, a driver superb.
>
> I praise the good driver,
> The road that he made,
> And hope you will never
> Be with him afraid.
> Out of the jaws of death!
> Back from the mouth of Hell!

A colorful comment was that of a rival stage driver, Bill Spiers, who lived to tell in his old age his recollections not only of Clark Foss but of the gaunt young Scotsman who came to Calistoga in 1880.

"Stevenson didn't lay it on none too thick," Spiers conceded in speaking of his skilled contemporary. "Colonel Foss weighed two hundred and sixty-five pounds, and could handle six horses like you'd handle that many cats. He would lift them right up off their feet and swing them around the corners so fast you couldn't see the leading team. He drove his stage to the Big Geysers for years, and he'd run down the last hill with a yell to wake the dead."

During the summer Stevenson spent in his county, Bill Spiers was hauling bark to a Napa tannery. He had eight mules and a "back-action," and hauled eleven cords at a time. Sometimes when he wasn't hauling bark he drove a rig for William F. Fisher, owner of the Calistoga livery barn. "And that's how I come to drive a rig for Stevenson," Bill explained. "I drove him up the mountain to the Toll House more than once! I didn't know he'd be so famous, or I'd have noticed him more particular. I remember one hot day he come over to the stage barn to hire me to carry him up the mountain. He'd walked down to Calistoga but he was too tired for the uphill climb. Well, I drove him up there to Silverado in a four-horse rig, trottin' the horses all the way so they was in an awful sweat when we got there; and I says to him, 'What the hell's your hurry?' Didn't seem to me he had so much to do that we had to race up the mountain. Fact is, I thought him kind of a fool, livin' in that old shack awritin' books! I wasn't much interested in books, nor didn't care to be. I was a few years younger than he was, but I didn't think he was hardly as smart as I which had got my diplomy back in Kintucky when I was seven and a half."

Stage robbing at that period in the development of the West was a regular business, and Napa County furnished an ideal setting. Not only Mount Saint Helena, but the canyons of the mountains to east and west provided hide-outs for bandits. Many of these were of course genuine desperadoes; but some were, or had been, quite respectable citizens—prospectors, merchants, anything—who succumbed to the lure of the express box with its rich spoils, and who probably enjoyed the "faint warfaring aroma" of the chase. The newspapers called them gentlemen highwaymen.

Black Bart, whose reign of terror covered the years 1875–83, was one of these gentlemen who frequently visited Napa County. Legend has it that his favorite hide-out was behind a huge fir on a rugged hillside, where the Lawley Toll Road overhung "a narrow and deep canyon filled with trees." Neatly dressed, gentle mannered, and well spoken, with a kindly face and humorous blue eyes, he was usually mistaken for a clergyman when off duty. With a bundle of blankets slung across his well-clad shoulder (there was a disjointed shotgun inside), he would appear at some farmhouse for breakfast, listening with grave headshake to the excited accounts of last night's stage robbery.

Unlike most of the other robbers, Black Bart (Charles E. Boles) was a lone wolf. No stage driver ever saw his face, but none who had glimpsed his crouching figure clad in a linen duster and surmounted by a flour-sack mask, or heard his deep bass voice crack out, "Throw down the box!" ever risked a personal acquaintance with his gun—which after all was a big bluff, for he never once used it, and claimed that it had never been loaded. When finally captured by a detective of the Wells Fargo Express Company at his rooming house in San Francisco, he proved to be as gentle as he seemed, as real a Jekyll-Hyde as Stevenson's fictitious one. A laundry

THE "CALIFORNIA" IN FRONT OF SPIERS' STAGE BARN

Courtesy Wm. Spiers

THE STAGE DRIVER, FOSS, LEAVING FOSSVILLE FOR THE GEYSERS

Courtesy Wm. Spiers

mark on a handkerchief lost at the scene of his one unsuccessful holdup proved his undoing. Until that fateful day in 1883, his crimes had paid off handsomely.

Clarence Myers, a contemporary of Clark Foss and Bill Spiers, often met Black Bart on his stage-driving trips across the mountain. Myers also had a long acquaintance with another gentleman, Buck English, who, he said, beat them all. "Buck was a likely appearin' young man; well educated, nice lookin', who would have passed in any society, though he carried on a stage-robbin' business for many years with great success." Holdups on Mount Saint Helena were common, and after a holdup there was always a hunt. "But my own business," Myers sagely added, "was drivin', so I stayed by the stage and let others chase the robbers."

Bill Spiers, too, often met Buck English. He said that Buck was a neighbor of the people he victimized, coming of a respectable family on the Lake County side of the mountain. He was captured in 1895, at the hands of a posse of Napa men. Like Black Bart, he was a model prisoner at San Quentin and was eventually paroled, but he died soon after, still in the prime of life, still a handsome, well-mannered "gentleman."

The author of *Treasure Island* took a most lively interest in the stage-robber stories that were current in 1880. Several found a place in *The Silverado Squatters*.

"Only a few days ago the Lakeport stage was robbed a mile or two from Calistoga. In 1879, the dentist of Mendocino City, fifty miles away upon the coast, suddenly threw off the garments of his trade, like Grindoff, in *The Miller and His Men*, and flamed forth in his second dress as a captain of banditti. A great robbery was followed by a long chase, a chase of days if not of weeks, among the intricate hill-country; and the chase was followed by much desultory fighting, in which several—and the dentist, I believe, amongst the number—bit the dust. The grass was springing for the first time, nourished upon their blood, when I arrived in Calistoga. I am reminded of another highwayman of that same year. 'He had been unwell,' so ran his humorous defence, and 'the doctor told him to take something, so he took the express box.' "

This express box contained wages for the miners of the Napa and Lake County quicksilver mines. The masked robbers or road agents were likely to time their holdups to coincide with payday; and in spite of the armed guards or messengers sitting aloft with shotgun in hand, they all too often got away with the spoils. Moreover, their spoils were usually worth while—gold dust, silver bullion, quicksilver flasks, often running into thousands of dollars.

In all the discussions of stage robbers, the people displayed a kind of waiting, an affectionate interest that yet held a hint of menace. Stevenson noted this two-edged tolerance with amusement. His neighbor on Mount Saint Helena, Rufe Hanson, qualified, he said, both as a hunter and as an amateur detective, and his attitude was the same toward both occupations. "It was he who pursued Russell and Dollar, the robbers of the Lakeport Stage, and captured them the very morning after the exploit, while they were still sleeping in a hayfield. Russell, a drunken Scotch carpenter, was even an acquaintance of his own, and he expressed much grave commiseration for his fate." Like the deer on the mountain, stage robbers were neighbors until they became game.

The Petrified Forest

It was a pure little isle of touristry
among the solitary hills.

STEVENSON was always more interested in people than in places. His readers remember the villagers, the inn-keepers, the wandering minstrels, when the country he traversed in his *Inland Voyage* and his *Travels with a Donkey* has long since blurred in their memory. They see Jones, the Welsh blacksmith, and other "elderly youths" who crossed the Atlantic with him, when his description of the *Devonia*, and even her name, are forgotten. They recall the emigrant train that carried him across the plains, but they recall it chiefly for the "chums" who shared its primitive accommodations. And to an even greater degree, because of the greater detail in Stevenson's descriptions of them, they remember the California pioneers who filled the pages of *The Silverado Squatters*.

The region of Mount Saint Helena, while geographically interesting, was to Stevenson primarily a background for his actors, the real-life actors who were the blood and sinew of this picturesque bit of California thirty years after the Gold Rush. There were the stage drivers and the highwaymen who captured his first interest, and the Calistoga hotelkeepers, Chesebro and Brannan, both forty-niners. There was Charley Evans, the "brave old white-faced Swede" living in the strange

37

forest of stone with the niece who afterward shared her pictures of him; Jacob Schram, the German winegrower, whose son never ceased regretting his indifference to a guest who was on the way to fame; Colin T. McEachran, Schram's nearest neighbor, whose letter regarding Stevenson's visit to his vineyard was to be treasured as history; and an unnamed rancher, informally identified as Frank McDonald, whose daughter later told about the day the dark-eyed Scottish stranger visited her childhood home in Knight's Valley. There was Morris Friedberg—"Kelmar"—the unliterary storekeeper of Calistoga, upon whose not too disinterested advice Louis and Fanny Stevenson chose Silverado as their temporary abiding place. There were Rufe Hanson and his pretty wife and stalwart sons, squatters at Silverado; there was the Guile family on the slope of Mount Saint Helena; there were the "seven sleepers of the Toll House"; there were miners who had gone, and mine owners who came that summer on mysterious business to the Stevensons' shabby abode. These people, to R. L. S., were actors in a pageant portraying frontier California.

The Petrified Forest was given the honor of a chapter to itself in *The Silverado Squatters*. But Stevenson was admittedly less interested in this geological wonder than in its owner, Charley Evans, whose real name was Charles Peterson, but who went by the local appellation of "Petrified Charley." "Sight-seeing," concluded the distinguished visitor, "is the art of disappointment, but fortunately Heaven rewards us with many agreeable prospects and adventures by the way; and sometimes, when we go out to see a petrified forest, prepares a far more delightful curiosity in the form of Mr. Evans, whom may all prosperity attend throughout a long and green old age."

The bride and groom made the trip during the first days of their sojourn at Calistoga, when they were still

"PRIDE OF THE FOREST" (PETRIFIED CHARLEY ON LEFT)

Courtesy Mrs. O. G. Rohl

MRS. ANNIE SCHRAM   JACOB SCHRAM

COLIN T. McEACHRAN

at the Springs Hotel and devoting some time to seeing the country.

Advertisements in the local papers of the valley told about the many wonders of the region. Guests were urged to visit the Napa and Lake County health resorts, the Big Geysers of Sonoma County, the Petrified Forest. To enhance the lure of the last-named attraction, some one of the owners who succeeded Sam Brannan at the Hot Springs Hotel had erected on the Spring Grounds a little grotto made of slabs of petrified bark taken from stone redwoods found in the wondrous place. Who would not want to visit the spot from whence came such unusual building material?

The forest lay in a deep canyon of the Mayacomas Range, dividing Napa from Sonoma County. There was at this time no direct stage line. Louis and Fanny must needs hire a rig to reach it. They followed a little-used mountain road through green timbered valleys, across splashing streams and over a sharp divide. Their driver, a "spectacled Swede," countryman to the owner of the forest, gave them a lesson on Western trees, pointing out differences in leaf structure between the madroña, the manzanita, the buckeye, and the maple. He showed them a group of young redwoods encircling the stump of the old. It was a perfect afternoon, late in May—the sun warm, the breeze cool—and all three enjoyed the trip.

"To the right or the left," observed Stevenson accurately, "there was scarce any trace of man but the road we followed; I think we passed but one ranchero's house in the whole distance, and that was closed and smokeless. But we had the society of these bright streams—dazzling clear, as is their wont, splashing from the wheels in diamonds, and striking a lively coolness through the sunshine. And what with the innumerable variety of greens, the masses of foliage tossing in the breeze, the glimpses of distance, the descent into seemingly impenetrable thickets, the continual dodging of the road, which made haste to plunge again into the covert, we had a fine sense of woods, and spring-time, and the open air."

At the top of the grade, before their final descent, they caught a noble view of Mount Saint Helena, from this angle a more majestic picture than from Calistoga, where they had seen but one spur of the mountain's huge bulk. Now they were viewing it from the north instead of the south, and all three peaks were outlined against the "blue hilly distance." The tangled wilderness that intervened between the mountain and the road was almost impossible to describe, even for so skilled a manipulator of words as R. L. S. It seemed that the country here had not been traversed since the volcano of Mount Saint Helena had spewed forth the stream of mud and ashes that had engulfed the redwood forest thousands of years before this day.

The five-mile drive from Calistoga ended abruptly at the foot of a sharp ridge of black tufa, crested with rock as white as snow. The driver of the rig from the livery barn turned to the right, through a gate with a wooden signboard. " 'The Petrified Forest. Proprietor: C. Evans,' ran the legend." Just inside the gate, on a little rise, stood a trim white cottage with a railed veranda, shuttered windows, and a big red chimney. A little farther up the winding road was a crude museum built by the proprietor when he discovered his petrifactions in 1871; and beyond this the Stevensons saw a pleasant bit of woods in which the cinnamon-red bark of manzanita, the smooth pale orange of madroña, and the gray twisted branches of live oak mingled their dark shadows.

Now Petrified Charley appeared, was introduced, and proceeded to escort his guests up the hill, on foot.

Suddenly they were in the midst of the "various lengths of petrified trunk," which Stevenson later described. Enclosed by wire fences, these bore mute testimony to the orgy of destruction that had laid them low. Torn, uprooted, thrown to the earth, they had given their fragrant branches to a great conflagration. And then their giant trunks, lying on a slant in two tiers, their tops all pointing away from Mount Saint Helena, had turned to stone.

Petrified Charley showed the guests his most wonderful treasure, "Pride of the Forest," a *Sequoia gigantea* twelve feet in diameter, with an oak of no mean size growing up through a crack in its trunk.

All very curious, thought Stevenson, "and ancient enough, if that were all." The heart of the geologist must quicken at the sight. As for himself, however, he felt a little bored. Presently he found himself contemplating not the petrifactions but their owner.

"He had wandered this way, Heaven knows how, and taken up his acres—I forget how many years ago—all alone, bent double with sciatica, and with six bits in his pocket and an axe upon his shoulder."

Before homesteading his acres he had been a sailor, then a prospector, and got no good from either. But this lonely place had hit his fancy and brought him luck. The climate, with a sea breeze every afternoon throughout the summer, had cured his sciatica, though he still hobbled a little as if in memory of it. His sister and his niece had come across the ocean to keep house for him, the niece teaching music up and down the Napa Valley. And then this "ranche," the spot he thought the most beautiful in California, had uncovered its petrified forest, bringing him a sufficient income from tourists' fees.

"A tardy favorite of fortune," thought Stevenson, smiling. All his sensibilities were on the alert. He was no geologist—he was a writer, a specialist in human nature. How transfer this man's individuality to paper? How describe him so that others would see him as he was? Fingers itched for notebook and pencil.

Fanny, on the other hand, was bent on statistics.

" 'Who first found the forest?" asked my wife.

" 'The first? I was that man,' said he. 'I was cleaning up the pasture for my beasts, when I found *this*'—kicking a great redwood, seven feet in diameter, that lay there on its side, hollow heart, clinging lumps of bark, all changed into grey stone, with veins of quartz between what had been the layers of wood.

" 'Were you surprised?'

" 'Surprised? No! What would I be surprised about? What did I know about petrifactions—following the sea?' "

And then he told his theory of how the forest had turned to stone, a theory in which he differed (with evident pride, said Stevenson) from all the scientific people who had visited the spot. Learned professors who came to examine the trees thought they had been borne to the ground by the weight of volcanic mud and ashes carried on a high wind, that they had lain in hot alkaline water under the mud, and that the silica in the water had changed their wood to stone.

Bah! Petrified Charley scorned any such notion as that. Why, the trees hadn't so much as "grewed" there! "He flung about such words as 'tufa' and 'silica' with careless freedom," but Stevenson never quite understood in exactly what details his theory differed from that of the scientists. Nor did it matter in the least. He wanted to know more about this man's background.

"When I mentioned I was from Scotland, 'My old country,' he said, 'my old country'—with a smiling look and a tone of real affection in his voice. I was mightily surprised, for he was obviously Scandinavian, and begged him to explain. It seemed he had learned his English and done nearly all his sailing in Scotch ships. 'Out of Glasgow,' said he, 'or Greenock; but that's all the same—they all hail from Glasgow.' And he was so pleased with me for being a Scotsman, and his adopted compatriot, that he made me a present of a very beautiful piece of petrifaction—I believe the most beautiful and portable he had."

The old man's niece was not at home on that memorable afternoon. Some of her music pupils lived so far away that she had to spend the night in Napa Valley, said her uncle. This niece later married O. G. Rohl and lived in Oakland, but in Stevenson's day she was known as "Petrified Lizzie." She and her aunt, "Evans's" sister, Christina Ryden, had come from Sweden during the previous year. Lizzie liked to show the photograph of the family group, taken in 1879 and illustrating Stevenson's description of the house of the proprietor of the forest with such fidelity that it might have been posed for his purpose. On the front porch was Mrs. Ryden. Seated just outside was old Charley with his pet goat. And out in the yard, where a great oak tree threw its shadow, stood Petrified Lizzie in Swedish costume, holding the bridle of the horse that carried her to her music pupils.

"My uncle's goat was the terror of my life," Lizzie Rohl used to explain, laughing. "He was always coming after me with his horns down! He was fond of chewing tobacco and would eat anything in creation. One day my uncle had a bucket of green paint out in front of the house and the goat ate every bit of it. You'd think that would have been the end of him, but he didn't seem to have even a bellyache."

She regretted not having met the visitor from Scotland. "But my uncle was awfully tickled about having met him—he made me feel real bad because I hadn't been there too."

With what genuine sorrow would Stevenson have learned that the old man went to his reward only a few months after that eventful day!

"Poor Petrified Charley (immortalized by Stevenson in his *Silverado Squatters*) went to San Francisco about 1880 and fell down the stairs of the hotel, from the effects of which he died (what a fate for a man that had sailed every ship and undergone a thousand dangers), and the haunt on the mountain top which knew him so long will know him no more. The visitors of bygone days will remember his quaint genius which presided over the forest, and the goat for which he was always ready to beg tobacco." So wrote his obscure biographer in an old county history.

Possibly Stevenson would be less "mightily unmoved" could he visit the forest today. The excavations have continued exposing more and more of the stone tree trunks over an area a mile long and a quarter of a mile wide. But since our visitor of 1880 never improved his lagging interest in geology, it is highly likely that he would again give his chief attention to some humble personage encountered there by accident.

Napa Wine

———◆◆◆▶———

A California vineyard, one of man's out-
posts in the wilderness, has features of
its own. There is nothing here to re-
mind you of the Rhine or Rhone, of
the low Côte d'Or, or the infam-
ous and scabby deserts of
Champagne; but all is
green, solitary, covert.

STEVENSON had not forgotten the view from the train
windows of the rich vineyards near the town of Saint
Helena. And so, when young Mr. Johnson, his landlord
at the Hot Springs, offered to show him the cellars of a
certain Mr. Schram, he accepted with enthusiasm.

In Johnson's trap on that bright May day were four
people—the innkeeper, the visitor from Scotland, young
Mrs. Johnson, and Fanny Stevenson. They drove down
the valley between oak-dotted meadows and wooded
hills. A short distance below Calistoga was an old grist
mill where they must stop for sight-seeing. The mill,
Johnson told them, had been built in 1846 by an English-
man, Dr. Edward T. Bale, owner of Rancho Carne
Humana. Stevenson was greatly interested in the
"enormous overshot water wheel as tall as the trees that
grow beside it."

Continuing their journey, they followed a mountain
road into the western hills, a road very similar to the one

that had led them to the Petrified Forest. After five miles of green thicket, watered by mountain streams, they saw two houses, one above the other in a "steep and narrow forest dell." These were the homes of two Napa County vintners, Colin T. McEachran and Jacob Schram, whose names (one of them misspelled) will survive as long as English literature.

"Mr. M'Eckron's is a bachelor establishment; a little bit of a wooden house, a small cellar hard by in the hillside, and a patch of vines planted and tended single-handed by himself. He had but recently begun; his vines were young, his business young also; but I thought he had the look of the man who succeeds. He hailed from Greenock: he remembered his father putting him inside Mons Meg, and that touched me home; and we exchanged a word or two of Scots, which pleased me more than you would fancy."

McEachran was as observant as his guest. Years later he put down in a letter his recollections of the conversation. Stevenson, he said, was enthusiastic about this region as a producer of wine, and predicted great future prosperity. "Evidently he had not yet heard of phylloxera. His remarks on the 'Glen' and other places shewed that he had an eye to observe and a genius to appreciate whatever is beautiful or grand in natural scenery. He was a thorough Scotchman and loved the rugged mountains and blinding mists of his native land —at a distance. I had no intimation at the time that he was a writer."

A niece of McEachran, Hannah Weinberger, who lived in an ornate Victorian house next door to the Weinberger cellars near Saint Helena, added her bit to this story. "Except that he misspelled the name, Stevenson's description is accurate," she said, bringing out a copy of *The Memorial and Biographical History of Northern California* to substantiate her claim. As recorded in this

46

RAILROAD STATION, CALISTOGA, IN SAM BRANNAN'S TIME

Old drawing, artist unknown (about 1871)

NAPA VALLEY FROM MOUNT SAINT HELENA TOLL ROAD

Photo, Redwood Empire Association

volume, Colin T. McEachran was born in Greenock, Scotland, in 1824, coming to America with his parents when he was seven years of age. He went to sea in his youth, became a captain and later a ship chandler, came to California in 1858, engaged in mining for a few years, and finally settled in Napa County, where he bought and developed Alta Vineyard. His cellar of native stone was but two years old at the time Stevenson inspected it.

The Memorial and Biographical History of Northern California contained a sketch also of the life of the second winegrower. Jacob Schram was a native of the Rhineland. Coming to America at the age of sixteen, he was for several years engaged in barbering in New York. During the Gold Rush he came to San Francisco via Panama, and continued his trade in various California towns, finally locating in Napa City. He purchased land for the Schramsberg Vineyard and planted fifty acres of vines, continuing his barbering itinerantly. His was the first underground cellar, dug into the side of a rocky hill. The house in which he entertained the Stevensons was a vine-covered brown cottage with a long veranda.

Here R. L. S. had a thoroughly good time. "His place is the picture of prosperity: stuffed birds in the verandah, cellars far dug in the hillside, and resting on pillars like a bandit's cave:—all trimness, varnish, flowers, and sunshine, among the tangled wildwood. Stout, smiling Mrs. Schram, who has been to Europe and apparently all about the States for pleasure, entertained Fanny in the verandah, while I was tasting wines in the cellar. To Mr. Schram this was a solemn office; his serious gusto warmed my heart; prosperity had not yet wholly banished a certain neophyte and girlish trepidation, and he followed every sip and read my face with proud anxiety. I tasted all. I tasted every variety and shade of Schramberger, red and white Schramberger, Burgundy

Schramberger, Schramberger Hock, Schramberger
Golden Chasselas, the latter with a notable bouquet, and
I fear to think how many more. Much of it goes to London—most, I think; and Mr. Schram has a great notion
of the English taste."

To his diary next day Stevenson confessed eighteen
varieties of Schramberger—with more than eighteen
flavors still mingled in his mouth.

Schram's vineyard was smaller than many. It contained only the choicest grapes, all except three thousand
of the sixty thousand vines being foreign varieties.
Jacob Schram, a painstaking vintner, as Stevenson smil-
ingly observed, had brought the knowledge of his art
from the famous Liebfrauenberg vineyard on the banks
of the Rhine, and his vintages, long before Stevenson's
tasting, were considered among the best in California,
making a reputation for him abroad.

"He is one of the most remarkable examples of success in the state," wrote a local editor five years before
Stevenson knew him. "He came here without money,
without credit, and without friends. He believed that the
highlands would far surpass the valley for wine making,
so he went far up, at great expense, where the clearing
of every acre cost him $150. There he made his home
and commenced his little vineyard, going on Saturdays
and Sundays to the White Sulphur Springs and to Calistoga, where, by acting as a barber, he obtained cash to
assist him in his enterprise."

His wife who so graciously entertained Fanny Stevenson, was, before her marriage, Annie Christine Weber,
of Worms, Germany. She was a worthy helpmeet, cheerfully bearing her full share of early hardships, directing
the vineyard when her husband was away barbering, enjoying with him the later years of ease and travel. The
couple had an only son, Herman, who was at home on
the day of the Stevensons' visit, but so absorbed in his

preparations for a hunting expedition that he failed to give the strangers a second glance—a circumstance he regretted in after years when Robert Louis Stevenson had become world famous.

In Saint Helena it was old Fanny Shamp who liked to supplement Stevenson's story of these vintners. "My father built a home in the valley in 1871, and Jacob Schram and Colin McEachran were our nearest neighbors. Mr. Schram was a typical German—fat, round-faced, good-humored—and his wife was a buxom and friendly *Hausfrau.* McEachran lived alone in the little cabin still standing on his place. He was a most upright, honorable man, esteemed and respected by everyone. I remember one incident that brought out these traits of his clearly. One dark night during the rainy season he was going into town on horseback, when his horse stumbled at the edge of a swollen stream not far from our house, and threw him, breaking his leg. Wounded as he was and suffering tortures, Mr. McEachran dragged himself up the hill to our front porch. He managed with a desperate effort to stand erect before he knocked. 'Seeing a man lying prostrate at your door would have been a shock,' he said. 'I wanted you to know at once who it was and what was wrong.' He was always like that, thinking more about others than about himself."

Prosperity for the Schrams and other vintners had one serious interruption. The dread pest, phylloxera, the scourge of European vineyards, was in 1880 beginning to show up in Napa Valley. A Calistoga correspondent to the *San Francisco Bulletin*, on February 26 of that year, wrote as follows: "I see the time will come, and it is not far distant, when all those splendid thrifty vineyards that are in a healthy, flourishing condition at the present time will be forsaken and devastated and dying with that terrible plague, the phylloxera." In the next decade destruction was almost universal. Then the

United States Department of Agriculture developed a resistant root stock, which was successfully grafted with cuttings of desired varieties, and by 1890 new vineyards were thriving where the old had been destroyed.

There were about fifty cellars in the county at the time of Stevenson's visit. The largest was that of Charles Krug. It measured ninety by a hundred and four feet, and was, like almost all the others, constructed of native stone, looking not unlike an old mill that had lost its mill wheel. Across the highway was Los Hermanos, another large cellar surrounded by a vineyard begun in 1876 by Jacob and Frederick Beringer. This cellar the Stevenson party visited. They followed a road through extensive gardens of tropical luxuriance, stopping before the two-story winery tight against the hill. Carpenters were at work adding a third story. Doors stood open below, and the visitors could look in on rows of casks stretching away in underground tunnels. An unmistakable odor of ancient vintages filled the air.

Jacob Beringer had been the foreman of Charles Krug's cellar. A native of the Rhineland, he recognized here a peculiar formation of limestone adapted to underground storing, common along the Rhine, but rare in the United States. Here, therefore, he built his winery, each floor being a single room with rows of stanchions as the only divisions. The third floor, to be used for crushing, had hatchways to conduct the juice to tanks below. The cellar, dug by Chinese coolies, had eight hundred feet of tunneling, the two main tunnels running two hundred feet into the hillside. These were connected by several laterals, so that the entire hill was honeycombed. The space underground was filled with oval casks of about six hundred gallons' capacity each. So tightly did the building hug the hillside that wagons could unload their grapes, at ground level, into the new third story at the rear.

Fine vintages, celebrated in song and story since the days of Homer, "imperial elixirs, beautiful to every sense, gem-hued, flower-scented, dream compellers," these appealed strongly to Stevenson's imagination. Here there was no quarrel between the Scotch Covenanter and the artist. Grossness was as impossible to his nature as teetotalism; wine was "bottled poetry."

At the time of his visit, the Napa County vineyards had already taken on many of the features of the European wine areas. This favored region of gentle Old World loveliness had a climate very similar to that of the best vineyard regions of Europe, with a moderate, even temperature, a rainless summer free from frosts, brilliant sunshine like southern France and Italy. Here was a light volcanic soil on foothills and mountain slopes, a porous gravelly soil along valleys, each suited to its own type of grape. Here were limestone cliffs and hills, soon tunneled out for storage of casks.

The wineries were the most noteworthy architectural features of the county. Their solid gray-brown walls, covered with ivy, had been constructed by European stone masons, out of "memorial stone" from the near-by hills. In architecture they borrowed from German *Schloss* and French *château*, familiar to the pioneers from Germany, France, Italy, and Switzerland, who comprised the bulk of the early vintners. These people gave up gold for grapes, turning to a new kind of prospecting, for which they had brought knowledge and aptitude from the Old Country.

The earliest vineyards were planted with the Mission grape, a small, blackish, inferior variety, carried over from the Spanish era of California history and grown for home consumption by the Spanish-Mexican and American settlers who lived in Napa Valley a decade before the Gold Rush. Father Junipero Serra, first missionary from Spain to Alta California, had planted the first cutting near San Diego in 1772. The vine took its name from the Missions strung like beads on a rosary along the Camino Real from San Diego to Sonoma, their vineyards planted and harvested by the Indians under the direction of the padres.

The poor quality of the Mission wine was believed to be due to the heavy irrigation considered necessary by settlers accustomed to summer rains in their home countries. At any rate, it was the experiments around Napa and Sonoma in the late 'fifties and early 'sixties that proved the superiority of high, light, dry soils for wine grapes. "Napa Valley," observed Stevenson, "has long been a seat of the winegrowing industry. It did not here begin, as it does too often, in the low valley lands along the river, but took at once to the rough foothills, where alone it can expect to prosper. A basking inclination, and stones, to be a reservoir of the day's heat, seem necessary to the soil for wine; the grossness of the earth must be evaporated, its marrow daily melted and refined for ages; until at length these clods that break below our footing, and to the eye appear but common earth, are truly and to the perceiving mind, a masterpiece of nature." In most other parts of California, high-lying vineyards were still experimental.

To Count Ágoston Haraszthy, a Hungarian nobleman who came to California from Wisconsin in 1849 and planted a hundred acres of imported vines on a dry hillside near Sonoma, belonged the credit for initiating this new era. His successful experiments attracted wide attention. In 1861 the Governor of California sent him to Europe to study winegrowing there, and he returned with over two hundred thousand rooted vines, representing hundreds of choice varieties. Napa Valley growers were quick to accept Haraszthy's aid. The first extensive vineyards to grow imported wine grapes were those of Charles Krug and Dr. George Belden Crane. In the next twenty years scores of growers throughout the county continued the experiments, trying out one foreign variety after another, about one hundred being found eminently adaptable to this region. The most popular in Stevenson's day were the Zinfandel, the Riesling, and the Chasselas. Some of the older wineries were even then world famous for their vintages and took prizes in competition with European wines.

Conjecture ran high as to the size of the 1880 grape crop. The *Saint Helena Star* predicted a fifty percent larger yield than in any previous year, remarking cheerfully that the phylloxera was working only in small areas. Stevenson was familiar with the havoc wrought by this pest in the vineyards of Europe, where there was more than a little reason to fear total loss. He "looked forward with a spark of hope" to the time when the wines of Napa Valley might take the place of those of Bordeaux; hence his deep interest in the vineyards of Schram and McEachran and Beringer.

His interest in Napa wine was to become part of local tradition. How fascinating to him, then a little-known scribbler sojourning in a little-known community, could his vision have taken him into the future, to a Vintage Festival in Saint Helena, where he was a personage in a pageant depicting the history of this county that now boasted itself the dry wine center of the world.

House Hunting

---◆•••▶---

One thing in this new country very particularly strikes a stranger, and that is the number of antiquities.

IT WAS RUMORED about the Spring Grounds that the sick Scotsman and his bride were moving to the Williams ranch, a snug summer retreat hidden away in a remote canyon of the Sugarloaf, on the Knight's Valley side of Mount Saint Helena. Stevenson's little milkmaid heard the story from her parents, and sadly anticipated the loss of her playmate.

Nor was the rumor unjustified. In letters of the period, Stevenson described a definite "ranche among the pine trees and hard by a running brook," where he and Fanny were to "fish, hunt, sketch, study Spanish, French, Latin, Euclid and History; and, if possible, not quarrel." The description of the mountain home and the list of occupations fit the Williams place precisely. And here, as things later worked out, the Stevensons and their artist friends, Virgil and Dora Williams, spent many happy hours during the summer, though most of the studying was left to Lloyd Osbourne under Stevenson's tutelage.

But although they frequently visited this woodsy "ranche," Louis and Fanny never actually shared the house. While they were still in San Francisco, Mr. and Mrs. Williams had told them about the ghost towns near their summer home. "It was with an eye on one of these deserted places, Pine Flat, on the Geysers road," said Louis, "that we had come first to Calistoga." His wife knew all about ghost towns. As the very young wife of another man, she had lived in the vicinity of Virginia City. She had heard many stories of miners deserting their cabins when the luck ran out. And these stories spurred the ready imagination of her new husband, the financially embarrassed Robert Louis Stevenson. "There is something singularly enticing," he wrote wistfully, "in the idea of going, rent-free, into a ready-made house."

Pine Flat, which a few years before had claimed several thousand inhabitants, was still a station on the Foss toll road. Surrounded by inactive quicksilver mines, the town consisted of three little houses, a boarded-up general store, and two hotels, only one of which, the Thompson House, was open to travelers.

This phantom place might indeed have provided a free roof over the head of Robert Louis Stevenson and the wife he was unable to support. But they must have food as well as a roof. Clark Foss, stopping at Pine Flat to change horses, could have delivered meat and groceries, but in those days, before refrigeration, he could not have been relied on for unsoured milk. Humorously, the city-bred invalid, for whom fresh milk was essential, considered buying his own cow. But this "would have involved taking a field of grass and a milkmaid," after which "it would have been hardly worth while to pause, and we might have added to our colony a flock of sheep and an experienced butcher."

And so there was an end to speculation concerning Pine Flat—fortunately enough, for shortly after midnight of a hot Sunday in July, Reeve's Hotel, Thompson's Hotel, and Thompson's store were burned to ashes, supposedly by incendiaries. It was impossible to save them, because the fire company consisted of two men, the entire number of inhabitants then in the town. Had the Stevensons become Pine Flat squatters, they might have lost what little they had in the conflagration. They might even have lost their lives.

Morris Friedberg, upon whose not too disinterested advice they became Silverado squatters instead, was Calistoga's pioneer merchant. A short, bearded Russian Jew, he was known about the countryside for his skullcap. Stevenson called him "the village usurer." There was a saying in Calistoga that he would get you in a corner if he could; and many legends were current concerning the extent to which he could "put on the screw." The Friedberg family, father, mother, and two sons, lived upstairs over the store, a two-story frame building on Lincoln Avenue, with a high false front carrying a signboard. The boys were musically inclined, Charley playing the violin and Fred the flute. Mrs. Friedberg helped her husband in the store and was said to be as "close" as he.

Perhaps it was because of the amount of space he gave to the account of Friedberg's unconscious spur to literature in finding him a dwelling place at Silverado that Stevenson bestowed upon this man the only actual pseudonym in *The Silverado Squatters*. His thrusts at the "Hebrew tyrant" were playful, and he took care to forestall any anti-Semitic interpretation on the part of his readers. "The whole game of business," he reminded them, "is beggar my neighbor; and though perhaps that game looks uglier when played at such close quarters and on so small a scale, it is none the more intrinsically inhumane for that. The village usurer is not so sad a feature of humanity and human progress as the millionaire manufacturer, fattening on the toil and loss of thousands, and yet declaiming from the platform against the greed and dishonesty of landlords." In those days, fifty years after the industrial revolution, manufacturing meant for city workers low wages, long hours, sweat-shop conditions. By comparison, Friedberg's rural "slaves" were well off.

It was doubtless on the occasion of a visit to the Calistoga store to make some trifling purchase that Stevenson had the conversation with the "tyrant" that resulted in his becoming a squatter at Silverado. "Now, my principal adviser in this matter was one whom I will call Kelmar. That was not what he called himself, but as soon as I set eyes upon him, I knew it was or ought to be his name; I am sure it will be his name among the angels. Kelmar was the storekeeper, a Russian Jew, good-natured, in a very thriving way of business, and, on equal terms, one of the most serviceable of men. He also had something of the expression of a Scotch country elder, who, by some peculiarity, should chance to be a Hebrew. He had a projecting underlip, with which he continually smiled, or rather smirked. Mrs. Kelmar was a singularly kind woman; and the oldest son had quite a dark and romantic bearing, and might be heard on summer evenings playing sentimental airs on the violin."

Three reasons were advanced by the storekeeper for the superiority of Silverado over Pine Flat: it was close to the Toll House, where the Lakeport stage stopped daily; there were near neighbors, the Hansons, who could be relied upon to deliver milk; and the climate was recommended as beneficial to consumptives.

Stevenson at once accepted the old man's generous offer to take him and Fanny house hunting at Silverado. From the back door of the store a fine view could be had of Mount Saint Helena and the site of the mining camp halfway up her great bulk. The silvery name of the place at once struck the writer's fancy; the location above the fog pleased him still more; and the fascinating history of the now deserted town sealed the bargain. "It was but a little while ago that Silverado was a great place. The mine—a silver mine, of course—had prom-ised great things. There was quite a lively population, with several hotels and boarding-houses; and Kelmar himself had opened a branch store, and done extremely well—'Ain't it?' he said, appealing to his wife."

It was eight o'clock of a bright June Sunday when the storekeeper, bound on an outing into Lake County, picked up the Stevensons at their cottage, the plan be-ing to drop them at the Toll House for the week end, and pick them up again on Monday morning. Besides Fried-berg and his wife, and their friend Abramina and her little daughter, the carriage contained a mysterious col-lection of coffee kettles, "highly ornamental in the sheen of their bright tin." These kettles, Stevenson discovered with amusement, were the coin with which Friedberg financed the outing. The people he was to call upon—at the Toll House, at Silverado, in Lake County—were enslaved to him by debt, and none would dare refuse when he forced them to buy a kettle, thus enslaving them still more.

The Lawley toll road struck off to the east, two miles out of Calistoga. It crossed a dry creek bed, wound its way along high cliffsides, reached its summit at the Toll House, and then plunged downward toward Lake County. Stevenson, in the rear seat of Friedberg's trap, enjoyed the ride immensely.

"The sun shone out of a cloudless sky. Close to the zenith rode the belated moon, still clearly visible, and, along one margin, even bright. The wind blew a gale from the north; the trees roared; the corn and deep grass in the valley fled in whitening surges; the dust towered into the air along the road and dispersed like the smoke of battle. It was clear in our teeth from the first, and for all the windings of the road it managed to keep clear in our teeth until the end."

A last look at Napa Valley as the trap rounded a sharp curve well up on the grade, and then the "vineyards and deep meadows, islanded and framed with thicket," gave way to primeval forest. As they neared the summit of the road, the little party could look down into King's Canyon on their right, the awe-inspiring towers of Cathedral Rock rising straight and high beyond its green depths. On the left the terraced slopes of Mount Saint Helena rose higher still, seeming to touch the sky. The sparkling air, the cool wind, the altitude, the resin-scented pines—all contributed to Stevenson's sense of verdant space and sunny gladness; and as the horses drew the trap up one steep slope after another, he felt that he was scaling heaven. Indifference had been left behind him in the valley.

The wind grew stronger. At the summit of the grade the little company came under its full weight. But this was the end; they had reached their goal. "At the highest point a trail strikes up the main hill to the leftward; and that leads to Silverado. A hundred yards beyond, and in a kind of elbow of the glen, stands the Toll House Hotel."

In years to come, skilled engineers would tear a path through these mountain spurs whose contours the winding, narrow toll road followed so pleasantly as it meandered in and out. A great stone highway, arrogantly bent on short cuts, would slice off the forward end of the Toll House croquet ground, leaving the inn stranded on a kind of island between the old road and the new. The inn itself would change its lines. But the toll bar, that rude barrier that held up all comers until they had paid their toll, would remain. Fastened to a tree, it would mutely remind visitors of the day when it did its duty in barring the way to wagons and stage coaches alike. And on the wall of the near-by tollkeeper's lodge, a little two-room house hard by the inn, the blackboard that was there in old days would continue to announce the rates of toll.

```
One-horse rig ........................50 cents
Two-horse team and wagon .............75 cents
Four-horse stage ...................$1.00
Six-horse stage ....................$1.25
Eight-horse stage ..................$1.50
```

On this early summer Sunday of 1880, Morris Friedberg brought his team to a halt in the shelter of the Toll House veranda. The little party climbed down from the high-seated carriage, and while Friedberg tied his horses, R. L. S. took note of his surroundings, his photographic mind recording each detail for future use.

"A water-tank, and stables, and a grey house of two stories, with gable ends and a verandah, are jammed hard against the hillside, just where a stream has cut for itself a narrow canyon, filled with pines. The pines go right up overhead; a little more and the stream might have played, like a fire-hose, on the Toll House roof. In front the ground drops as sharply as it rises behind. There is just room for the road and a sort of promontory of croquet ground, and then you can lean over the edge and look deep below you through the wood. I said croquet *ground*, not *green*; for the surface was of brown, beaten earth. The toll-bar itself was the only other note of originality; a long beam, turning on a post, and kept slightly horizontal by a counterweight of stones."

Friedberg led the way into the bar, where Stevenson was introduced "to Mr. Corwin, the landlord; to Mr. Jennings, the engineer, who lives there for his health; to Mr. Hoddy, a most pleasant little gentleman, once a member of the Ohio legislature, again the editor of the local paper, and now, with undiminished dignity, keeping the Toll House bar."

The description of these three was supplemented in later years by Mollie Patten, wife of the erstwhile superintendent of the Phoenix Mine and daughter of the man who built the toll road. Aunt Mollie came as mistress to the inn six months after Stevenson left the mountain, and she was always ready to add her postscript to his story.

"Lewis Marion Corwin," she said, "was a Hoosier, but he had been in California many years. He was book-keeper at my father's Banner Warehouse in Napa City, then landlord at the Toll House, and later went into real estate in Los Angeles. He was popular with the guests while here—full of the devil and always up to tricks.

"Mrs. Corwin was Annie D'Arcy, a local woman. Her portrait used to hang in the parlor, as Stevenson describes it.

"Frank Jennings is politely called a mining engineer, but about all the mining he ever did was to draw a check from his father once a month. He was the son of John D. Jennings, Chicago millionaire, sent West for his health. He used to go fishing sometimes, but mostly he sat around in the bar or on the porch, the way Stevenson says.

"G. P. Hoddy published the *Calistoga Free Press* for about a year and a half before he became barkeeper at the Mountain Mill House and later at the Toll House. He was a neat, dapper, so-so little man, slim, dark, with curly hair, always telling jokes and stories."

The editor who succeeded him at Calistoga described Hoddy as "full of vim and go-ahead activeness." He had started from Nashville, Tennessee, with fifty cents in his pocket, worked for nine months in Kansas, and arrived in California with a little more money than he'd started with, becoming editor of the *Calistoga Free Press* during the mining excitement that built Silverado. Shortly after Stevenson moved there, Hoddy was promoted to full charge of the Toll House, while Corwin was engaged as census enumerator for the district.

After a great deal of handshaking in the bar—to

Stevenson "too considerable a familiarity to be squandered upon strangers"—the Friedberg party set out for Silverado, a little boy from the hotel guiding them up the hill. The road where the mine carts had run was still plainly marked, and this led them to an open plateau on the southeast side of the mountain. "That was the site of Silverado mining town. A piece of ground was levelled up, where Kelmar's store had been; and facing that we saw Rufe Hanson's house, still bearing on its front the legend, Silverado Hotel. Not another sign of habitation. Silverado town had all been carted from the scene; one of the houses was now the school-house far down the road; one was gone here, one there, but all were gone away."

Rufe had fled his creditor's coming, but his wife directed the house hunters farther up the mountain to Sam Chapman's old boardinghouse, adjacent to the mine. Here they might find living quarters.

They followed the road that had been Silver Street, until it came to a sudden end at the foot of an ore dump twenty to thirty feet high. They could see the iron chute extending from the outer edge of this rampart, where the miners had poured gold and silver ore into mule carts waiting to carry it down the mountain to the stamp mill. By means of a wooden ladder and a rocky path, the house hunters reached the top of the dump, part of which was covered by a triangular platform. Stevenson was amazed to find a mass of old wood and iron—as though the place had been deserted only the day before. There was a railroad track that ran from the chute to the mine shaft and from there to the tunnel far back in the canyon. One little ore car still stood on the track. Forward from the shaft, on the western side of the platform, was a weather-brown wooden shed built against a boulder, shaded by madroñas. Under the shed was a blacksmith's forge. On the opposite side of the platform, braced by a much larger boulder, was another weather-brown building—Chapman's bunkhouse for miners.

This bunkhouse was in three sections, each in reality a separate cabin, and each a little farther up the hill. The broken door of the first, on the level of the dump, opened to the south, with a view of green trees. There was but one room, about thirty feet deep, the rear wall tight against the "bold, lion-like red rock" that overhung the triple-tiered building. This room had been the office of the Silverado assayer, Professor John O'Leary. His heavy pestle, a foot square, was still part of the litter of the platform.

The apartment above could be entered only by means of a board propped against the threshold. It opened to the west, with a view up the canyon. The room was much larger than the one below, and contained eighteen bunks.

In order to reach the third cabin or room, it was necessary to find the path that led upward behind the big rock. The door was level with this higher ground, the room extending back upon the hill. Inside were the uprights for more miners' bunks. This had been a dormitory set aside for Chinese miners, and Stevenson christened it "the Chinaman's house."

From here the party could look down upon the main shaft of the mine, which they now proceeded to investigate. The staging that held the windlass was still intact, and from the top they could look into the open pit. Stevenson noted a trickle of water and a stray sunbeam. A tunnel bit into the ledge westward. Rufe Hanson's wife, who had accompanied them, suggested that Mrs. Stevenson could keep her milk and butter in this tunnel, a capital refrigerator. "Wine, too," thought R. L. S.

"Close by, another shaft led edgeways up into the superincumbent shoulder of the hill." In order to reach it, they must all scramble up a steep slope, thickly strewn with fragments of ore, beautifully tinted—red, yellow, brown, and black from iron, blue-gray where the veins of silver ran, and sparkling white with quartz crystals. At last they reached a wide, level floor of solid rock, with a second ore chute at its outer edge and another tunnel piercing the mountain at its rear. A cold dampness met them at the mouth of the black cavern which Stevenson called the "horizontal shaft." Even when seen across the canyon, this broad gash in the ledge had been impressive. Close up, it was still more awesome. Deep into the mountain, pick and blasting powder had torn at the vein of ore, and the opening had been wedged apart with heavy beams, called in the language of the miners "stulls."

Following the others once again to the platform, Stevenson stood looking at the oddly shaped miners' barracks. He had expected something like an English cottage on a green. Instead, all was rust and decay. The view up the canyon was one of desolation. Yet the view in the other direction was of green trees, and the house, he had to admit, could be made habitable. His mind was made up: "Silverado be it!"

The decision was a triumph for Friedberg, who now led the way back to the Toll House, with many admonitions to be ready for the return to Calistoga by six o'clock on Monday morning.

It was ten o'clock instead of six, however, when the merry party drew up at the toll bar after the week end, and there was a further delay while the last of the coffee kettles was forced upon the unwilling Corwin—Stevenson meanwhile keeping the horses quiet by quoting to them as much French poetry as he could remember.

Off at last; but when they were not a mile down the mountain they must stop at the Guile ranch. Stevenson told the story querulously, giving, as usual, his own spelling to the family name. "Only the old lady was at home, Mrs. Guele, a brown old Swiss dame, the picture of honesty; and with her we drank a bottle of wine and had an age-long conversation, which would have been highly delightful if Fanny and I had not been faint with hunger." Then Mr. Guile came in from the vineyard, delaying the journey further but offering Stevenson a chance to order a supply of Mission wine, to be stored away in the tunnel at the mine when he moved into the bunkhouse.

It was two in the afternoon when the "pallid" house hunters arrived on the Spring Grounds. Lunch at last, a bit of rest, and they began their preparations for moving to Silverado, their own private kingdom, reluctantly accepted but soon beloved.

The King and His Kingdom

——————◆••◆——————

*There were four of us squatters—myself
and my wife, the King and Queen of
Silverado; Lloyd, the Crown
Prince; and Chuchu, the
Grand Duke.*

LOUIS STEVENSON's friends and many of his readers
never ceased wondering how he could have chosen an
abandoned mine as a site for squatting. Nellie Sanchez,
who visited him and Fanny on the mountain, expressed
this attitude in her biography of her sister: "The old
bunkhouse seemed to me an incredibly uncomfortable
place of residence." Margaret Stevenson voiced a similar opinion when her wandering son returned to Scotland. She couldn't quite accept Fanny's laughing statement that they had spent a jolly summer.

That Louis did enjoy camping out in this unaccus-
tomed spot, where "mountain and house and the old tools
of industry were all alike rusty and down-falling," was
clearly enough indicated in his letters and in the Silverado chapters of his new book. They were his favorite
chapters, and he called them "belles pages."

Nellie Sanchez might have found one clue to the attraction Silverado held for him had she followed the
path he took daily from his cabin to the Toll House. On
the day he took possession he chose this short cut through
the woods when he went after hay for bedding.

66

"Signs were not wanting of the ancient greatness of Silverado. The footpath was well marked, and had been well trodden by thirsty miners. And far down, buried in foliage, deep out of sight of Silverado, I came on a last outpost of the mine—a mound of gravel, some wreck of wooden acqueduct, and the mouth of a tunnel like a treasure grotto in a fairy story. A stream of water, fed by the invisible leakage from our shaft, and dyed red with cinnabar or iron, ran trippingly forth out of the bowels of the cave; and, looking far under the arch, I could see something like an iron lantern fastened on the rocky wall. It was a promising spot for the imagination. No boy could have left it unexplored"—much less the author of *Treasure Island!*

His mind must have gone back, as he stood here, to that episode of his childhood described in *The Lantern-Bearers*, when a group of his young friends stole away at dusk to an old ten-man lugger in the cove, each with a bull's-eye lantern buttoned under his coat. One of these friends, in Miss Masson's *I Can Remember Robert Louis Stevenson*, wrote that these secret meetings were entirely Louis' idea, and that he entertained the other lantern-bearers with tales of pirates, smugglers, and hidden treasure.

It may well be that the idea of *Treasure Island* was conceived in this happy moment of rediscovered boyhood before the treasure grotto of Silverado. Stevenson, the writer, was storing his mind with characterizations and descriptions to be used in future stories—and *Treasure Island* is especially rich in transferred Silverado scenes.

The attraction of the old mine did not end with his discovery of the treasure grotto—which to anyone else was an abandoned miners' tunnel, denoting failure. The forge, the chutes, the shafts, the great gaping seam in the cliff, the ruin of the dump, the weather-beaten house, the very bunk he slept in, made the same appeal to his romantic imagination. He who later conjured up John Silver and his motley crew for the amusement of his stepson had no trouble reconstructing Silverado's past glory for the pleasure of that same boy, and himself as well.

It was as King of Silverado that he took possession of his rusty realm; and the wreck of a house that so distressed some of his friends was a palace. In *The Silverado Squatters* he presently told how he and his wife and his dog set out from Calistoga in a double buggy. The date was June 9, a Wednesday. Lloyd Osbourne, who had recently come from San Francisco, rode ahead on a pony, probably his mother's Clavel. Rufe Hanson was to follow with bags and boxes and a second-hand cookstove. Most of the boxes contained books, which to R. L. S. were more necessary than rugs and furniture.

The royal party picnicked at noon at the old stamp mill, a pendicle of their mine, halfway up the mountain, where a few years back the gold and silver had been extracted from the ore. Here was another rich spot for the imagination, another old brown building which now stood deserted, the sunbeams striking on rusty, silent machinery through chinks in the wall.

Rufe Hanson was delayed by a game of poker, and while they waited for their belongings, after they had "been landed" at the mine, Louis and Fanny set to work, cleaning house. They began on the lower cabin, which was to be their dining room and kitchen. Here they found "a table, a barrel; a plate-rack on the wall; two home-made boot-jacks, signs of miners and their boots," and a pair of papers tacked to the boarding, the new squatter misreading their headings, for they had to do with two tunnels of the mine, not two "funnels!" The floor was deep in debris, but without a broom they could scrape out only the rougher part—stones, bits of wood, straw, and paper.

Paper! Scraps of ancient newspapers, from the years when the mine was turning out riches; and billheads of the Chapman boardinghouse, some headed Silverado, some Calistoga Mine.

Louis, groping among the scraps, tucked away a sample billhead, to be kept with other relics of the summer and brought out of hiding when he came to write *The Silverado Squatters.*

Calistoga Mine, May 3d, 1875

John Stanley
> To S. Chapman, Cr.

To board from April 1st, to April 30 ....$25.75
” ” ” May 1st to 3d 2.00

———
27.75

"Where," he wondered, "is John Stanley mining now? Where is S. Chapman, within whose hospitable walls we were to lodge? The date was but five years old, but in that time the world had changed for Silverado." Ah, to find a letter, a notebook, a diary, a ledger, a list of the boarders' names, a file of whole newspapers, anything to tell the story of the past! Again the romantic imagination was on fire. Louis Stevenson, groping about on his knees for research material, was less novelist than historian.

His hope that Stanley or Chapman might read his account of their "anterior home" was later realized. Both men were living in the Calistoga region when the book was published, and when every literate person in the community read it, if only to find his name. Sam Chapman, in particular, would have been only too glad to answer Stevenson's plaintive query as to his whereabouts. He had lived in Calistoga for eleven years. Before landlording the Silverado bunkhouse, he had worked as a carpenter and operated a small wagon factory on Lincoln Avenue. He had owned several successive pieces of property and now lived in a ranch house on the Saint Helena highway.

While Louis, that afternoon, lost himself in the past, Fanny was thinking more practical thoughts. This old assayer's office was no bridal bower, to be sure, and after the Springs Hotel it seemed crude indeed. But Fanny never engaged in self-pity. This was not the first difficulty she had faced. She had lived through a variety of heart-wrenching experiences—married as a mere girl to a lovable but unstable man; taking her children to Europe when that marriage was going on the rocks; losing there, among strangers in a strange land, her cherished little Hervey; violently drawn to the scribbler of Grez, and drawing him in turn across an ocean and a continent; nursing him through the gravest illness of his life, and finally marrying him, sure that he would live but a few months more. She had faced these problems, not always with equanimity, but with a courage the equal of Louis Stevenson's own.

This unpromising dwelling was another challenge; it cried aloud to be transformed by a few feminine touches into a cozy summer nest. Miners' cabins were no novelty to her. Back in Nevada, where Sam Osbourne was prospecting when she joined him in the West, she had lived in a house more primitive than this. Her front room, carpetless and curtainless but clean, had contained only her wood-burning cookstove, a table, and a few chairs. What miner's wife had more?

Here there was already a table, and Rufe Hanson was bringing the cookstove Louis had bought at Calistoga. As for chairs, they weren't needed. When she had unpacked their clothing and books, she would up-end the trunks and packing boxes and use them for seats and cupboards. Homely household inventions were her delight; she would have enjoyed comparing notes with the castaway Swiss Family Robinson. Fanny Stevenson was a genius at homemaking under difficulties, and in many parts of the world thereafter, wherever life led her health-seeking mate, she again set to work, with pluck and fortitude and imagination, to create from the materials at hand a home.

The materials offered her at Silverado were crude but sufficient. "Wood, iron, nails and rails" were strewn about the platform. From old boots left in a dog hutch near the forge she planned to cut hinges for the sagging kitchen door. White cotton cloth from Friedberg's store could be tacked across the windowless window frames. Upstairs, the door by which the royal family went in and out was whole; the bunks only needed to be filled with sweet-smelling hay from the Toll House barn, and then made up with her Oakland sheets and blankets. And as for the third-floor apartment, that was to be a playroom for the Crown Prince. Here his printing press was to be installed when it arrived; the toy printing press on which the boy had already run off the first number of *The Surprise*. Louis wanted to see in print the poetry he had been writing in San Francisco and Oakland, and maybe some little stories that could be illustrated by means of wood blocks. Little did Fanny guess that the following winter that printing press would go with them to Davos in the Alps, and that in future years its quaint products would sell for many pounds sterling each!

While his wife planned the house, Louis found some practical work out of doors. With pick and shovel left by the miners, he "deepened the pool behind the shaft." The stream that came out above the Toll House roof had been tapped by the shaft of the mine, and ran underground until it emerged below the treasure grotto to seek its old channel. Its source was a spring near the upper cabin "where Chinamen had slept." From this spring a rotten wooden trough led the water down behind the shaft into what was now Louis Stevenson's back yard. Smack under the hill, at the lower end of the trough, it fell into a tiny pool.

Louis was in the midst of a dense thicket of the varied shrubbery of the mountain, breathing the sweet fragrance of the showy white azalea and the modest maroon-petaled calycanthus. It was a pleasant spot; later he would come here for exercises and sun baths. But now to work! The pool was shallow; he must make a well by digging it deeper and then lining the circular wall with a masonry of pebbles.

This was a task requiring time and patience. Today he merely dug down a bit. In leisurely days to follow, he would fit one smooth flat pebble against another, pressing them gently into the damp earth until his miniature of masonry was finished, to stand into distant years, a small and perfect record of his very human self.

Summing up his first day as a squatter, he later said, "It required a certain happiness of disposition to look forward hopefully, from so dismal a beginning, across the brief hours of night, to the warm shining of tomorrow's sun." That happiness of disposition, fortunately, he had, but it was sorely tried before Rufe Hanson and his wagon arrived, long after dark. The sun had already set behind the mountain when the new squatter returned from his well-digging. In the kitchen Fanny had no stove and no supper to cook. A chill was in the air, now that it was growing dark. Future writing, future housekeeping were forgotten; what they wanted now was light, fire, and food.

Fanny's was probably the inspiration that led to their holding their housewarming around the blacksmith's forge across the platform. Here they soon had a good fire going—"fire, which gives us warmth and light and companionable sounds, and colours up the emptiest building with better than frescoes," as Louis later wrote. They sat about in the blacksmith's shed, each finding an impromptu seat—a rock, or a log, or a broken beam. "For awhile it was even pleasant in the forge, with the blaze in the midst, and a look over our shoulders on the woods and mountains where the day was dying like a dolphin."

This, throughout the summer, was to remain Louis Stevenson's favorite corner. The morning sun never penetrated the cool shade of the madroña thicket that surrounded the low, brown building. With his back propped against the blackened boulder that would mark the spot long after the forge and shed were gone, he could look out over the edge of the dump on the green world below. Here, during working hours, he wrote. In the afternoon, when the westering sun was striking hot against the bunkhouse, the forge and the madroñas were still in the shade, and this was his social corner. Evenings he sat here looking at the stars. Many a night he strolled about the platform, watching the dawning of those stars and pitying his fellow humans who never enjoyed such a pleasure, because they always lived in houses. The rest of the family would be in bed, "and even from the forge" he could hear their sleepy voices.

Twice, in writing up his notes, he described this favorite spot. "If the platform be taken as a stage, and the out-curving margin of the dump to represent the line of the footlights, then our house would be the first wing on the actor's left, and this blacksmith's forge, although no match for it in size, the foremost on the right." And again, "Only in front the place was open like the proscenium of a theater, and we looked forth into a great realm of air, and down upon treetops and hilltops, and far and near on wild and varied country. The place still stood as on the day it was deserted . . . . a blacksmith's forge on one side, half buried in the leaves of dwarf madroñas; and on the other, an old brown wooden house."

When seven o'clock came on their first night at Silverado, it was decided that Louis must descend the canyon to the Toll House to buy a loaf of bread. He set out with a lantern they had found in their barracks and was successful in his quest. On the return trip, however, he lost Lloyd's watch, entrusted to his pocket for safekeeping, and had to retrace his steps. Within sight of the lighted windows of the inn, he miraculously found the watch in the middle of the footpath—but the final climb uphill cost him more than he could afford in the way of physical strength. When he arrived at the top of the dump he was "broken with fatigue" and must pay the price in pain.

Long after dark Rufe Hanson arrived and brought his wagon to a halt at the foot of the ladder that led up to the dump. With him were two of his wife's relatives, ready to lend a hand with the moving. Where there had been firelight and reverie, suddenly all was action. The three men carried box after box into the assayer's office that was to be the kitchen. They brought the stove, but it was impossible to put it up before the morrow because they had forgotten the stovepipe and lost a lid. The squatters spread out a bit of supper to eat with the Toll House bread, but it was a cold supper, even the fire in the forge being out.

The crew must have their own supper before they brought the bedding hay from the Toll House. But at last this too arrived, and two bunks on the second floor were made up. By candle light under the stars, the King, the Queen, and the Crown Prince made their way gingerly up the narrow wooden board that was their only stairway to that second floor. Through the doorless doorway and the windowless window frame the starlight came in "like mist." After they were in bed a high wind sprang up, a wind like that of their first night on the mountain, when they had slept at the Toll House. It was off among the trees, not with them in their canyon. So closely was their house planted under, around, and above the bold red rock, that they were protected from the gale. In their airy bedroom they were "fanned only by gentle and refreshing draughts."

Sleep came at last, even to the ailing King. The royal family had settled in the palace. Tomorrow in bright sunlight they would finish their unpacking and put up the stove. They would clean and repair the house and make it a home. When they had accustomed themselves to the change in their lives, they would find themselves "among the happiest sovereigns in the world."

Silverado

---◆◆◆◆▶---

No one could live at Silverado and not be
curious about the story of the mine.

THE Calistoga Gold and Silver Mine had its ambitious
beginnings eight years before Stevenson spent his honeymoon "in the wreck of that great enterprise." It resulted
from the fourth wave of mining fever to sweep Napa
County. In 1848 almost every male citizen had rushed
off to the Mother Lode to dig gold, many returning with
treasure. Ten years later, in the winter of 1858–59, the
same men hurried into their own mountains to dig silver.
At night myriad campfires lighted the eastern Mayacomas ridge. There was much strife about claims—but
only worthless ore resulted. Then came the quicksilver
excitement that brought lasting wealth to many. Cinnabar was discovered on the slopes of Mount Saint Helena
and in Pope Valley, and soon many mines were going full
blast. And while these were developing, there came the
final rush that uncovered both silver and gold and built
the town of Silverado.

In 1872 Alexander Badlam of Calistoga staked claim
to six thousand feet of the Monitor ledge on the southeast slope of Mount Saint Helena. He organized the
Calistoga Mining Company and took into partnership
Archibald Borland, Coll Deane, Thomas Reynolds, and
several lesser lights. These men opened a mine directly

behind the Toll House Hotel, about five hundred yards west of the toll gate.

Thomas Reynolds was the only member of this "Big Four" personally known to Stevenson, who in *The Silverado Squatters* called him "Ronalds," though he spelled the name correctly in his notes.

During the time the squatters occupied the company-built barracks at the mine, this "town gentleman" and another paid a visit to Silverado, inspecting the shafts and the several tunnels. Reynolds' remarks threw much light on the history of the venture, until then a mystery to Stevenson.

The date was June 27. The Stevensons and their guest, Joe Strong, husband of Fanny's daughter, were enjoying the evening in their outdoor parlor, when suddenly the two gentlemen came up the path. There was an exchange of good evenings, and then Reynolds led the way—magisterially, said the embarrassed R. L. S.—toward the lower shaft and the western tunnel that opened directly behind it, the tunnel set aside for the squatters' food and wine.

"Presently we heard his voice raised to his companion. 'We drifted every sort of way, but couldn't strike the ledge.' Then again: 'It pinched out here.' And once more: 'Every miner that ever worked upon it says there's bound to be a ledge somewhere.' "

These remarks identified the man beyond a doubt. Stevenson, who "liked well enough to be a squatter when there was none but Hanson by," felt deeply humiliated in the presence of this owner of his squatter's kingdom. He, the lord of Silverado, saw himself for once as a shabby beggar who must house his family where he had no right to tenancy.

Now Reynolds was extolling the past glory of the town. Silverado, he said, "was the busiest little mining town you ever saw," with a population of a thousand to

77

fifteen hundred. This information the eavesdropping Stevenson had been unable to get from his neighbors. Some good might yet come of the unwelcome visit. He made mental notes as Reynolds' story progressed, and later wrote it down.

"Ninety thousand dollars came out; a hundred and forty thousand were put in, making a net loss of fifty thousand. The last days, I gathered, the days of John Stanley, were not so bright; the champagne had ceased to flow, the population was already moving elsewhere, and Silverado had begun to wither in the branch before it was cut at the root. The last shot that was fired knocked over the stove chimney, and made that hole in the roof of our barrack, through which the sun was wont to visit slug-a-beds towards afternoon. A noisy last shot, to inaugurate the days of silence."

At the time he made this visit of inspection, Reynolds was preparing to prospect the lost ledge at its lower end, deep down in King's Canyon. Moreover, he was going to reopen the old stamp mill which Stevenson claimed as an appendage to his kingdom. The people of Calistoga would soon be able to set their clocks by the mill's cheery whistle. These plans were not disclosed to the listening squatters, though they were probably already known to the kid-gloved gentleman who listened as silently as they to Reynolds' story.

For weeks Stevenson had been speculating about the mine and the town. In his favorite outdoor nook under the shade of the madroñas near the forge, he had let his mind go back to the time when all was noise and bustle, "with a grand *tutti* of pick and drill, hammer and anvil, echoing about the canyon; the assayer hard at it in our dining room; the carts below on the road, and their cargo of red mineral bounding and thundering down the iron chute."

A true picture, but incomplete. The lord of Silverado

never learned the half of the Silverado story. At its peak, the newspapers called this Napa County gold and silver rush "an old-fashioned forty-niner excitement," so furious as to "start prospectors with sledge hammers, spades and pick axes, out with lamps, in a cold drenching rain." The whole Mount Saint Helena region was involved. Along two or three miles of its length in the direction of Knight's Valley, the Monitor ledge was pockholed with mining locations, as were its sister ledges, and an observer viewing the mountain from that side found it impossible to count the excavations of the miners.

A graphic description of the excitement was later given by Colin T. McEachran, the Scottish vintner whom Stevenson so greatly liked. In a letter to Thomas J. Pilkington, a newspaperman, McEachran wrote as follows:

I was of the prospectors who sought a new Eldorado about Mount Saint Helena in its palmy days and was for some time a boarder at Hotel Chapman and for aught I know may have snored as vigorously as John Stanley himself.

Those were busy, bustly days. Men with pick and hammer on the flanks and shoulders and crown of old Saint Helena, big with hope of the fortune which never came. Others were camped on Silverado flat and dug and delved in tunnels and gulches for the precious ore which "was there sure, if you could only strike it." Bespectabled professors who held forth in learned discourse of dips and spurs and angles, of porphyry and quartz and "indications." The Calistoga mine back of the Toll House was then in full blast and huge wagons loaded with quartz rumbled to the mill some three or four miles below to dump their loads to be pounded and ground and tortured till the rock yielded up its precious metal.

The news spread rapidly along the Pacific Coast. Men hurried in from all directions. Pine Flat, in its first boom, was almost deserted. Mountains several miles to the east and west of Mount Saint Helena were now prospected in the frenzy for silver, and even more for the "glitter of real free gold." It was the old story of 1858–

59 repeated—frantic digging by day, myriad campfires at night.

The core of all this activity was the Calistoga Gold and Silver Mine in the canyon above the Toll House Hotel, then newly built by William Montgomery, an old sea captain. A crew of forty-five men ran tunnels, dug out shafts, and hauled ore to the stamp mill, mules drawing the carts along a winding road that grew impassable at the height of the rainy season. About twenty tons of rock were crushed each day, most of it from the lower tunnel—Stevenson's treasure grotto—which started on the line of the ledge, at that point some thirty feet high, and ran straight into the steep bluff that formed the divide of the mountain.

The Silverado stamp mill, built in June 1874 at a cost of twenty thousand dollars, was three-quarters of a mile south of the summit of the toll road. It stood in a little mountain meadow within full view of Calistoga, the first ten-stamp mill for the reduction of gold and silver ore in the Coast Range. The foreman had worked in Nevada mills and declared that the Silverado ore compared favorably with that taken from the Comstock mines. Stevenson described the mill as "a great brown building, halfway up the hill, big as a factory, two stories high, and with tanks and ladders along the roof."

The mill was producing ten thousand dollars per day in bullion, and as the hopes of the promoters rose, they dreamed of a metropolis. Alexander Badlam drew a plan for a town and hired a surveyor to make a map and go to work. His was to be no mushroom mining camp, growing up haphazardly; his was to be a city deliberately laid out and as deliberately named.

On Sunday, October 11, 1874, a christening ceremony was held, with speeches and champagne. At three in the afternoon about a hundred people gathered under the shade of a big oak in what was to be the center of town.

They were high on a plateau on the south side of the mountain, seven miles north of Calistoga. Below lay the Napa Valley, where the christening party could see four towns, Calistoga, Saint Helena, Yountville, and Napa. Some of the people had come from those towns, some from Knight's Valley on the west, some from Pine Flat, a few from San Francisco. Aleck Badlam, who had succeeded Archie Borland as superintendent of the mine, greeted those assembled. He announced that the town they had come to christen was to be named Silverado. He predicted that it would be the second Virginia City. Already it was distinguished, for it was located "nearer the top of a mountain than any other town in the State, and closer to Heaven than sinners usually get." By the time the speakers who succeeded him had finished their extravagant prophecies of the wealth and greatness to come, everyone was a little giddy, and the meeting broke up in merrymaking.

On October 24, the *Napa Register* carried an interesting story: "A map of the new mining town, Silverado (late Borlandville) of the Mount Saint Helena mines, drawn by W. A. Pierce of this city, as surveyed by him October 16, 1874, was today filed for record in the office of the County Recorder. Messrs. William Montgomery, John Lawley, and William Patterson are designated as proprietors.

"The plan represents a wild, scraggly, stragglinglooking town, on the side of a mountain, with the grade from the Calistoga mine down to the Railroad winding through it, and the streets darting off at all angles, after the fashion of the early Spanish surveys. The thoroughfares of this new metropolis bear the high-toned names of Fifth Avenue, Garnet, Pearl, Ruby, Gold and Silver, while only two come down to such commonplace designations as Main and Market. The survey represents 282 lots in 13 different blocks, and will apparently accommodate the business of Silverado for some time to come. 'Surely there is a vein for the silver and a place for the gold where they fine it.'"

At the time of the filing of the map, the unfinished town had some forty or fifty inhabitants living in tents. Building lots, most of them twenty-five by a hundred and fifty feet, were staked out and numbered. Surveyors were working on the streets, which were sixty feet wide. The whole side of the mountain from below the inn to the eastern boundary of the Calistoga Gold and Silver Mine had been laid out, some of the streets running straight up the mountain.

A month after the christening the *Register*'s Calistoga correspondent, who signed himself Bret, predicted that "there can be no doubt but this is destined to be the greatest mining district on the Pacific." The boom was on. There was disparaging talk of Nevada's Comstock ledge. It was believed that Silverado's Monitor ledge would prove far richer.

Late in November, Robert L. Thompson opened the Silverado Hotel. It stood north and south in the center of town, shaded by a huge madroña. Its front door was at the gable end, facing Gold Street. While most of the boarders were miners, the hotel catered to all and sundry. Its first advertisement appeared in the *Calistoga Free Press* the day after Christmas. "Silverado Restaurant, Silverado, Saint Helena Mountain, R. L. Thompson, Propr.—The undersigned wishes to inform the traveling public and citizens of Silverado, and the mining camps around, that his Restaurant is now open and that he will be pleased to attend to their wants. Attached to the Restaurant is a Comfortable Saloon where the best wines, liquors and cigars can be obtained, and every politeness shown to patrons.—R. L. Thompson."

Before the turn of the year there were seven or eight business houses in the vicinity of the hotel, among them

THE TOLL HOUSE

Drawing, 1876, by Agnes Ray Sanders

THE UPPER SHAFT, CALISTOGA GOLD AND SILVER MINE

Photo by I. C. Adams

several of the inevitable mining-town saloons. Morris Friedberg had opened his branch store. A blacksmith was being sought. House lots were in great demand, and several fine dwellings were nearing completion. Aleck Badlam had a downtown office. Mining claims, undeveloped, were selling for twelve thousand dollars cash. Seventy men were employed at the mine, twenty at the mill. The town was developing according to plan, and already it had had its first murder.

Franklin Headley, a miner, had missed a bottle of whiskey and suspected that Scotty McDonald had stolen it. "On the morning of November 11, 1874, quite early, he went to the house where Scotty lived and called him out to shake hands with him. As they clasped hands, Headley dealt Scotty a furious blow on the head with a heavy instrument which he held concealed in his left hand, from the effects of which the man soon expired."

It was a rough life, and the men who day after day entered the tunnels and descended the shaft found little glamour in it. Their one strike for better wages and working conditions was quickly broken by a shutdown. Only by staking a claim and going out as a lone prospector could one savor the excitement that drove the big fellows who owned the mine.

Not all of the miners batched or boarded on Silverado Flat. About seventy-five were fed at Sam Chapman's "upper boardinghouse," a quarter of a mile beyond the outer reaches of the town. This boardinghouse was one of the first structures at the mine, dating from January 1874, when Badlam built his reduction works. Sam Chapman, whose bill for John Stanley's board had so puzzled R. L. S. on the day he moved into the three-tiered building, charged a dollar a day for board and bunk, with a neat reduction by the month. The board bills found by Stevenson were the last to be issued here. They were dated May 3, and covered the month of April. Chapman had bought the Silverado Hotel, and by May 15 had succeeded R. L. Thompson there as host and landlord, taking his boarders with him. O. P. Hoddy, then editor of the Calistoga paper, paid him a visit and reported everything clean and neat. "Mr. Chapman and lady do everything in their power to make their guests comfortable."

Chapman's last advertisement appeared in the *Calistoga Free Press* on June 26, 1875. In October Hoddy's paper failed because of the failure of the mine. During the summer there had occurred the frantic "drifting" described by Thomas Reynolds in the conversation overheard by Stevenson. A hopeless business; the ledge had been cut off by a fault. At last the company gave up, the miners left, and all the buildings except the hotel were moved from the Flat.

The proud little town of Silverado was never to revive. What had been the center of its active life remained "a lawn, sparse planted like an orchard, but with forest instead of fruit trees." Except for such parts of Main Street as coincided with the toll road, and for the upper part of Silver and the lower part of Market where the carts had run, the wide streets were obliterated. The stakes that had marked the building lots rotted away under the trees. In future years (when Mollie Patten sold these acres) there was a house and barn where the Hansons had lived. But never again would there be a mining town.

Even Stevenson's palace, the upper boardinghouse, was destroyed. What was left by curiosity seekers after *The Silverado Squatters* came out was moved to the level of the lower tunnel, his treasure grotto. Here it became a blacksmith's shed, housing a second forge. And then finally even this was destroyed in a forest fire that swept down the canyon.

Backwoods Neighbors

———————◄••►————————

*To be a gentleman is to be one all the
world over, and in every relation
and grade of society.*

THE LORD of Silverado, despite his vain efforts to separate fact from fiction when he quizzed his neighbors
about the history of the mine, did have an inkling that it
had not lived its last days. For he was present when Rufe
Hanson jumped the claim.

Thomas Reynolds had held that claim in the name of
the company during the previous year. There had been
much talk of jumping on the part of Rufe before this
great man's visit on June 27; and Stevenson was not a
little disturbed when Reynolds did not that very night
take steps to hold his property. He expected the man to
at least mention a piece of paper reposing on a cairn of
rocks high up behind the upper shaft; for it was by means
of this piece of paper that his property rights had been
protected. Already the time had passed for the renewal
of the claim, and the month's grace would expire in three
more days. But Reynolds did nothing.

The three days passed, the time was up, and Hanson
had done nothing, either. Then, a week after Reynolds'
visit, Rufe, his wife, his several sons, and the boarder,
Jim Breedlove, arrived at the Stevenson domicile, all
in their Sunday's best, Rufe carrying a roll of papers in
his hand.

Under the madroñas by the forge, the little company settled down, Rufe and his boarder gravely smoking, Mrs. Hanson volubly entertaining the Stevensons. At last the host, well aware that this visit had to do with the business of the mine, led the way to his barrack, Rufe following him up the shaky plank. Upstairs, the two men spread the papers on the little bedroom table. There were two sheets of clean white note paper, and a printed mining notice, dated May 30, 1879, much the worse for wear. This was the notice by which Reynolds had held the claim during the past thirteen months, and which had now run out. It was to be twice copied, in Robert Louis Stevenson's handwriting, one copy to be placed on the same cairn where Reynolds' now worthless notice had reposed, the other to be filed for registration with Sam Chapman, who, unknown to R. L. S., had recently been appointed mining recorder for the Calistoga district.

At last the deed was done; the claim was jumped. Yet, after it was all over, the scribe confessed, "I never had a glimmer of an idea what was going on!"

The legal basis for this transaction was the law of 1872, regulating the working of mining claims. On every claim located, until issuance of a patent, a miner was required to do a hundred dollars' worth of work or make a hundred dollars' worth of improvements each year. In case he failed to comply, the mine became subject to relocation.

Mollie Patten, after 1881 mistress of the Toll House, declared that Stevenson gave a verbatim account of the jumping that left him so puzzled. "The mining company," she explained, "due to a disagreement among themselves, did not come to do their hundred dollars' worth of assessment work that year, and their claim lapsed. Reynolds knew he couldn't hold the mine. He probably knew when he came inspecting, that night of June 27, that Rufe expected to take it.

"Rufe never worked the mine, and his claim lapsed, too. When Rufe's year was up, my husband, Dan Patten, did the jumping. He had been superintendent of the Phoenix Quicksilver Mine, and after we moved to the Toll House and bought five hundred acres up here, he wanted to own the Calistoga Gold and Silver Mine. So he took out a government patent—that is, he had the land surveyed and paid for it. He organized the Silverado Mining Company and spent some three thousand dollars strengthening the old workings. The mine was worked for several brief periods; then the claim lapsed again, and it was relocated and incorporated as the Mount Saint Helena Mining Company, after which there were two or three more short working periods."

Rufe Hanson's chief business was prospecting, and he had filed mining notices on many other strips of mountainside besides the one R. L. S. helped him seize. Nor was the Calistoga claim his last. Less than a year after the scene in Stevenson's barracks, he filed for registration in the Napa County courthouse the papers for a mine he named the "Palase."

Perhaps it was the hope of gold rather than silver that attracted Rufe and kept him digging on Mount Saint Helena. For he was a true pioneer of the California Gold Rush. When he was fifteen, he crossed the plains with his family. At the height of the gold fever, his father, his father's seven children, and the aunt who had brought them up, started out together from Ohio in a covered wagon. There were so many of them, however, that Rufe was crowded out. He rode horseback when a horse was available, and the rest of the time he walked. Stevenson must often have heard this story.

Father and sons became prospectors in the region of Placerville, and from there Rufe, his brother Bill, and his sister Nancy (who had married Gabe Conner, a hunter and guide of local renown) drifted into Napa

County with the many who came during the silver excitement of 1858–59.

Every man in the county, whether an old-timer or one newly arrived for the occasion, had his try at the local diggings unless he was physically disabled. Rufe was one of those who never gave up. He was still at it when the second silver rush began in 1872 with the formation of Badlam's company. He was living on Mount Saint Helena during the hectic early days of prospecting there. He saw the beginning and the end of the town on the flat, and when Sam Chapman gave up the Silverado Hotel, Rufe took it over.

His niece, Mrs. Lucy Ann Cole of Calistoga, called him happy-go-lucky. He was quite a hand with the violin, she said, and used to fiddle for the dances at the Silverado Hotel on Saturday nights. When the mine was abandoned and the village disappeared almost overnight, he remained as the sole householder of the once busy town, living free of charge in the hotel of which he had been landlord. He had several horses, a cow, a few chickens, plenty of wild game, and a whole mountainside to prospect. What more could a man ask?

"Uncle Rufe lived easy," Mrs. Cole would say when Stevenson's readers asked about him. "He never got excited. A really good man. Everybody liked him. Not that he didn't have a hand for poker, and a pretty little horse he ran sometimes in the Spring Grounds races."

According to her spelling, his name was Hansen— Rufus Hansen. (Stevenson's first spelling was Hansome; his second, Hanson.) Rufe spelled the name with an "o," his brother Bill, who lived on Windwhistle Mountain west of town, with an "e." The family was of Swedish extraction. There was money on his mother's side, but because of a feud over religion on the part of his uncles, Rufe never got any of it. Not that he really cared. Wealth, said his niece, just didn't come his way.

88

He was well known to both Mollie Patten and her brother, Charley Lawley, at the Toll House. Aunt Mollie described him as "a tall, lean, raw-boned hunter and trapper; shrewd, clear-brained, but without schooling; quiet in all his ways."

He was still prospecting around in his dreamy sort of way, she said, when she and her husband bought their five hundred acres on Mount Saint Helena in 1884. The property included the site of the mining town and the Silverado Hotel where Rufe still lived as a squatter. The hotel was to be moved down the hill to replace the Toll House that had burned, so Rufe left the mountain, never to return. He and his wife, his sons, and his brother-in-law drifted across the Sierra into Nevada, where there was endless room for prospecting, and where, a few years later, Rufe Hanson died.

When *The Silverado Squatters* was published he was still on Mount Saint Helena, and both Mrs. Patten and Mrs. Cole thought it quite likely that he chuckled over the description his neighbor squatter had written of him. "Most Calistoga people read the story when it first came out," said his niece. "That's when Uncle Rufe read it, I think; and though I was just a young girl, that's when I read it myself."

Stevenson, too, must have enjoyed that description. "In all that he said and did, Rufe was grave. I never saw him hurried. When he spoke, he took out his pipe with ceremonial deliberation, looked east and west, and then, in quiet tones and few words, stated his business or told his story. His gait was to match; it would never have surprised you if, at any step, he had turned round and walked away again, so warily and slowly, and with so much seeming hesitation did he go about. He lay long in bed in the morning—rarely, indeed, rose before noon; he loved all games, from poker to clerical croquet; and in the Toll House croquet ground I have seen him toiling at the latter with the devotion of a curate. He took an interest in education, was an active member of the local schoolboard, and when I was there, he had recently lost the schoolhouse key. His waggon was broken, but it never seemed to occur to him to mend it. Like all truly idle people, he had an artistic eye. He chose the print stuff for his wife's dresses, and counselled her in the making of a patchwork quilt, always, as she thought, wrongly, but to the more educated eye, always with bizarre and admirable taste—the taste of an Indian. With all this, he was a perfect, unoffending gentleman in word and act. Take his clay pipe from him, and he was fit for any society but that of fools. Quiet as he was, there burned a deep, permanent excitement in his dark blue eyes; and when this grave man smiled, it was like sunshine in a shady place."

Mollie Patten's brother, Uncle Charley Lawley, had his bit to add to this description.

"At the time Stevenson knew him," he said, "Rufe was, of course, a squatter like himself. The mine was idle and all the miners had moved away; nobody was interested in the old hotel, so he squatted there, paying no rent. He lived mostly from hunting. There was plenty of game, free for the taking. All that was necessary was to be able to hit it, and Rufe was a crack shot. He was always in debt to old Friedberg for what food he couldn't get with his gun, but that didn't worry him much. He made a little money from game, selling most of what he didn't use to Corwin. Two and a half dollars for a medium-sized buck was good pay. Corwin liked Rufe, and the two used to hold shooting matches out in front of the Toll House to see who could hit a target on one of the trees.

"I lived over in Pope Valley then, where my father owned stock in the Phoenix Quicksilver Mine. At stage time I'd come up to the Toll House for the mail, and that's when I'd see Rufe.

"I went hunting with him and some of the other men hereabouts several times, stopping by for him at the Silverado Hotel. We'd take the trail that led back through the canyon to the top of the mountain, passing Stevenson's cabin."

The local newspaper had for years kept tally on the number of deer slain during each hunting season by this "mighty hunter." In 1878–79 the total was seventy-two; in 1879–80, a hundred and fifty. The season opened July first, and Rufe was starting a new count at the time he told his friend, R. L. S., that he would greatly like a picture of himself in his buckskin hunting suit. It was to be a genuinely artistic composition, "with the horns of some real big bucks, and dogs, and a camp on a crick." Joe Strong, he thought, might like to draw such a picture.

Stevenson's liking for this man did not extend to his voluble wife. He thought her commonplace, comely though she was, with beautiful teeth and a good figure. "Her noisy laughter," he complained, "had none of the charm of one of Hanson's rare, slow-spreading smiles; there was no reticence, no mystery, no manner about the woman: she was a first-class dairymaid, but her husband was an unknown quantity between the savage and the nobleman."

Lucy Ann Cole agreed: "She was as noisy as he was silent."

Charley Lawley was more tolerant. "She was just as Stevenson pictured her," he said, "more than ordinarily handsome and always wearing a print dress and a sunbonnet. She was outspoken, but the soul of kindness." He added biographical details. "Her maiden name was Mary Jane Lovelands, and she was born in Napa. Her father was a carpenter who raised not only houses but also a large family of children."

Despite the extreme uncertainty of prospecting as a means of livelihood, Rufe and Mary Jane were not without hospitality. Jim Breedlove, who had witnessed the relocation papers and helped place one of them on the cairn of rocks, had crossed the plains in the party of Rufe's father. He lived for awhile with the family, as idle as his host. More permanently, Mary Jane's younger brother, Irvin (Stevenson spelled the name with a final "e") was housed with them as a sort of adopted boarder in an ex-hotel.

Irvin, though "beautiful as a statue," was even less given to work than his brother-in-law. Stevenson, usually so kindly, described him with a pen dipped in acid. "I do not think I ever appreciated the meaning of two words until I knew Irvine—the verb, loaf, and the noun, oaf; between them, they complete his portrait."

The woodpile beside the palace was the result of the oaf's much-prodded efforts. They must have firewood for their second-hand cookstove, so on the very first morning, while husband and wife were patching doors and windows, making beds and seats, transforming their rude dwelling into a home, Stevenson engaged Irvin as a woodcutter at so much per day. The youth appeared promptly, but all he did was sit and laugh and spit. After a few days the exasperated employer was driven to dismiss him. Then occurred an amusing interview in the bare north room of the Silverado Hotel. Stevenson, "with merely affected resolution," declared himself ready to chop his own wood. This was too much for the Hansons, who needed the lad's hire. They promised better behavior if Irvin was again employed, and Stevenson relented, adding when he wrote up the story, "The promise, I am bound to say, was kept."

Rufe was less egoistic than Irvin, and he had one genuine skill, his hunting. He was as thorough a craftsman in his hunting as R. L. S. was in his writing. But what chiefly endeared him to Stevenson was his touch of imagination. Thoroughly rural, discriminately idle, he was at the same time keen and thoughtful, with a poet's love of nature and a "fine, sober, open-air attitude of mind." Stevenson would have been surprised but not displeased to have heard Charley Lawley say, "Robert Louis Stevenson looked much like Rufe Hanson." Both men were tall, rangy, and thin-chested.

One of his London acquaintances once referred to Stevenson's appearance as that "of a Western back-woodsman." Stevenson's neighbors that summer were backwoodsmen in very truth. They were hardy sons of pioneers, and they accepted him as strangers are accepted in a pioneer land, on face value, no questions asked. Knowing nothing of his own world, they gave him no hero worship. When they noticed him at all, they thought him a sick-looking, quiet chap, who whiled away hours of enforced idleness (which surely he would have preferred to spend fishing or hunting) scribbling nervously in his everlasting notebook.

How amazed they would have been, these neighbors who liked him well enough as a plain human being, could they have known how keenly he was observing them while seemingly engrossed in writing, how many descriptions of them were being transcribed in that notebook, how their brief acquaintance with this queer scribbler was to save them from obscurity!

One of the Mount Saint Helena neighbors, Charley Lawley, was, like his friend, Rufe Hanson, a hunter "living really in nature." He was a Californian of the old days, of the prospecting, hard-drinking, stage-coach days; knowing the roughness and hardness of pioneer life, but knowing too the beauty of forests and mountains and flowering plants, of starry heavens and fog oceans.

When, like other Napa Valley folks, Uncle Charley

read *The Silverado Squatters*, he appreciated especially the chapter on "The Sea Fogs." He too had seen the Napa Valley when it seemed, from the mountain, an ocean, and he liked to give his own description of the scene, all unconscious of the simple beauty of his phrases that resembled Stevenson's own.

"At daybreak," he said, "the fog lies perfectly quiet, like water in a calm. When the sun comes out, it begins to move and climb. Mountain peaks and hills are islands until the fog moves higher and blots them out. Napa Valley on the east and Sonoma Valley on the west at last fill up, and all the islands are gone. And then if you climb higher up the mountain you look out over rolling billows. The hotter the sun, the more motion in the fog, you know. On a very bright day, the peak of Mount Saint Helena is reflected as though in a sea. Before such sights an old man like me takes off his hat."

Had Stevenson known Uncle Charley a little better (in 1880 a man younger than himself), surely he would have left a picture of him in *The Silverado Squatters*, for this man, too, was a poet.

Literary Work at Silverado

If I have faltered more or less
In my great task of happiness;
If I have moved among my race
And shown no glorious morning face;
If beams from happy human eyes
Have moved me not; if morning skies,
Books, and my food, and summer rain
Knocked on my sullen heart in vain:—
Lord, thy most pointed pleasure take
And stab my spirit broad awake;
Or, Lord, if too obdurate I,
Choose thou, before that spirit die,
A piercing pain, a killing sin,
And to my dead heart run them in!

IN THOSE quiet weeks at Silverado, resting after his almost fatal illness, with his beloved always near and with the sights and scents of the mountainside healing body and mind, Stevenson turned often to poetry, in the mood of lover and nature worshiper. The above lines from *Underwoods* are credited to this summer, not in their completed form, but roughly sketched under the title, "Indifference." They tell the story of the transition that took place at this period in Stevenson, the writer.

The year in California (August 7, 1879, to August 7, 1880, the dates of his sailings from Glasgow and New York) marked Stevenson's emergence into adulthood.

He was among strangers in a strange, indifferent land. For the first time he was cut off from his family. In San Francisco he was poverty-stricken, ill, face to face with realities for which his protected youth never prepared him. Under these conditions it was to be expected that the young man going on thirty should mature, not over-night, but in the course of one eventful year—the year, moreover, of his marriage.

Stevenson took his marriage very seriously. He had never been self-supporting, and the acquisition of a wife and a family under the conditions existing at the time laid a burden upon his heart and mind, which, together with the breakdown in health from which he never fully recovered, grew at last too heavy to be borne. From then on he was, in all seriousness, writing to earn a living; writing, too, with an interested, able, dictatorial critic by his side. As a writer, this summer at Silverado he left behind his fumbling youth.

Silverado was the retreat that healed his soul and gave him back to the world. In the hard months at Monterey and in "yon distressful city beside the gates of gold," he had faltered very seriously in the "great task of happiness," which had been and always remained the most characteristic tenet of his philosophy. Years before, in *An Apology for Idlers*, he had laid down his belief in "the duty of being happy," not for self, but for others. In this summer of peace and rest and sunshine, with books and enough of simple food, and "beams from happy human eyes," he grew able to take up his life where he had almost left it off.

His mood that summer was lyric, and it is very likely that the notebook, which the people at the Toll House— just as the friends of his youth—came to associate with his daily presence, recorded even more verse than it had in the preceding months. Much, of course, was discarded, but some found place in either the old poems or the "new." Graham Balfour listed the following verse as belonging to the year 1880.

"It is not yours, O mother, to complain," *Underwoods*, Book I, xxv.

"Not yet, my soul, these friendly fields desert," *Underwoods*, Book I, xxiv. Published in *Atlantic Monthly*, October 1880.

In the States: "With half a heart I wander here," *Underwoods*, Book I, xxix.

The Scotsman's Return from Abroad: "In mony a foreign pairt I've been," *Underwoods*, Book I, xii.

To Doctor John Brown: "By Lyne and Tyne, by Thames and Tees," *Underwoods*, Book II, xv.

The last two poems belonged to Scotland and the later months of the year. The others belonged to California, in their initial stages to San Francisco and Oakland, but reworked and reworded as was the way of R. L. S. The earliest version of his best-known poem, the "Requiem," also belonged to California.

Most of the lyric work of that year was not known to Balfour. It was gathered together years after Stevenson's death by the Bibliophile Society of Boston and privately published under the title, *New Poems*.

Before Stevenson journeyed to America he had already published twenty-eight or thirty of his best essays, five short stories that were later famous, and the two books of travel that preceded *The Silverado Squatters; An Inland Voyage* and *Travels with a Donkey*.

The greater part of his writing time while at Silverado was spent on his voluminous notes for the new book of which he had written Colvin while still at Calistoga. This was, of course, *The Silverado Squatters*. Earlier he had written the same friend, "Thence, as my strength returns, you may expect works of genius. I always feel as if I must write a work of genius some time or other; and when is it more likely to come off, than just after I have paid a visit to the Styx and go thence to the eternal mountains?"

He was, however, disappointed in the final product. Finished three years after his enthusiastic beginnings, revised and reworked, dropped during times of illness, taken up and reshaped when he was feeling better, "Silverado," he said gloomily, "is an example of stuff worried and pawed about, God knows how often, in poor health, and you can see for yourself the result: good pages, an imperfect fusion, a certain languour of the whole. Not, in short, art."

In an unhappy hour at Hyères he almost destroyed the manuscript, as he confessed in a letter to Jules Simoneau of Monterey. "Disgusted with my 'Silverado' story, of which I've made little that satisfies me, and doubly unlucky in just letting fall and smashing a gallon of 17th-century Cognac de Charente, I came near to destroying after all, the rubbish (drogue) of that crude miner's shack I wanted you to see, when in somewhat of its glory, and most likely would have done so, had not F., at the critical moment, come in and rescued the papers—which may prove was well or quite as ill!"

Fanny herself in that time at Hyères is said to have destroyed one of his manuscripts, an unfinished novel dealing with "Mary," a woman of the streets. By its break with Victorian tradition, this novel, had it been published, might have launched R. L. S. as a pioneer of the realistic school of storytellers. Fanny's domination had its fortunate as well as its unfortunate side, however, and in the case of the Silverado manuscript, the world is indebted to her for her interference.

The Silverado Squatters, as a piece of sincere reporting, was a great improvement over the previous travel books. Yet early critics shared the author's lack of enthusiasm, complaining that *The Silverado Squatters* had less vivacity and charm than the *Inland Voyage* and *Travels with a Donkey*.

Later critics were to reverse this judgment. John A.

MAP OF SILVERADO, 1874

Hall of Records, Napa County. Photo by Burrell Wilson

TABLET ERECTED ON THE SITE OF STEVENSON'S CABIN

Photo by I. C. Adams

Steuart expressed the opinion that the worrying and pawing about had clouded the author's judgment. "Stevenson," he said, "was taking the first decisive step in the difficult, and, as it might seem, the distasteful task of getting away from himself. Writing 'with his eye on the object,' he made a simple, honest attempt to describe things as he found them in that strange frontier existence into which destiny, as by a freak of satire, flung him. And he succeeded. The picture he gives of Silverado is a picture of reality, a piece of realism that may be called French in its precision."

Frank Swinnerton underscored this gain in realism, and pointed out that it resulted from a gain in character. *The Silverado Squatters*, he said, marked "the emergence of a new Stevenson," chastened, experienced, matured. The steerage journey to America, the hardships on board the emigrant train, the financial worry, the mental conflicts centering in his emergence from adolescence, the uncertainty of his future, finally his tussle with death—these were maturing experiences. Swinnerton added the significant statement that "those of us who never take these voyages out into the unknown, who sit tight and think comfortably of such things as emigrant trains, cannot realize with what sudden effect the stubborn impact of realities can work upon those who actually venture forth."

Stevenson himself was well aware of the changes wrought not only in his character but in his writing by his venturing forth into the adult world. "My head went round and looks another way now," he wrote to Henley; and later he expressed the same thought in a letter to Colvin: "I know my mind is changing; I have been telling you so for long; and I suppose I am fumbling for the new vein." That new vein was realism. He knew he was on the right track, but in the case of *The Silverado Squatters*, his perspective was thrown out of focus at the moment of completion of the manuscript. He was wearied and depressed by the grinding toil of his revision upon revision—for he was never a quick worker, and grinding toil was his lot.

Napa Valley people were among the first readers of the serial version when it was published in the *Century Magazine* in November and December of 1883. The American edition of the complete book was published by Roberts Brothers of Boston in December 1883, and Chatto and Windus published it at the same time in London. Some of the most fascinating chapters from the point of view of local history were omitted from the magazine version—parts of the chapters "Calistoga" and "The Return," all of "Napa Wine," "The Toll House," and "Episodes in the Story of a Mine"—but these were included in the book.

There is nothing to indicate that Stevenson contributed to the Calistoga newspaper, as he did to the *Monterey Californian* in the previous year. The *Calistogian* (successor to the *Calistoga Tribune* and the *Calistoga Free Press*) was three years old at the time of his visit, a lively and prosperous little journal under the editorship of J. L. Multer. The owner of the *Tribune* had brought his printing press around the Horn from New England, upon hearing from an acquaintance that there was a good chance for an editor here, and Calistoga had ever after been a good newspaper town. Since the name, Robert Louis Stevenson, had meant nothing to the editors of the San Francisco papers, it is not surprising that it meant nothing to the *Calistogian*. Nor is it surprising that the writer saved his sketches for his book.

At the time he wrote his description of Calistoga high street, Stevenson had not yet met Mr. Multer, but he undoubtedly met him later. He knew Charles A. Gardner, editor of the *Saint Helena Star*, and paid a visit to the *Star*'s printing office, where he was photographed reading galley proof. The *Star* had installed a new printing press, and this may have been the occasion of the visit.

During the summer at Silverado, Stevenson did a certain amount of revision, of course, on work begun in Monterey and San Francisco, putting in four or five hours of literary effort each day. The events of *The Amateur Emigrant* and *Across the Plains* were still fresh in his mind, and as it was his custom to work upon several manuscripts simultaneously, taking up whichever suited his mood, he must have given some attention to these and to the essays and fiction of 1879–80—"Some Aspects of Robert Burns," "The Story of a Lie," "The Pavilion on the Links," "Prince Otto," "Yoshido Torajido," "The Old Pacific Capital," "A Modern Cosmopolis," "Dialogue on Character and Destiny Between Two Puppets." The final version of *The Emigrant* was mailed at Calistoga. The essay on Thoreau, written at Monterey and San Francisco, was published in the *Cornhill Magazine* while he lived at Silverado.

He continued, too, the autobiographical notes begun in San Francisco, though the autobiography was never to be finished. Letters to his friends were conspicuously absent, in contrast with the voluminous ones he wrote from Monterey and San Francisco, and this is one reason for the meagerness with which his biographers reported the summer in Napa County. The recording of his experiences went into his notes for *The Silverado Squatters* rather than into letters. With his wife safely at his side, he needed less the solace of writing to his friends. There were letters to his parents, of course, both on his part and Fanny's. The wife wrote diffidently to prepare her parents-in-law for her coming. Louis' own letters must have been of a tender and contrite nature, after the recent reconciliation and the generosity of his oft-tried father and mother.

"I am allowed to do nothing," he wrote his mother.

But this statement, which seemingly misled some of his biographers, did not mean that his artist's mind had ceased functioning. Will H. Low, the American painter who knew him at Grez during his courtship days, once said that the idleness of which R. L. S. was accused at school and among his friends was an "industrious" idleness. If he wasn't off in a corner with his notebook, he was storing his mind with images, impressions, memories. "His mind was a treasure house." In his own youthful essay in defense of idlers, Stevenson himself remarked upon the amount of wisdom to be had by an intelligent person "looking out of his eyes and hearkening in his ears." And Rosaline Masson, his discerning Edinburgh biographer, said with regard to his egoism, "To the artist the *esse* of things is not what they are, it is the *precipi*—it is what effect they produce on the artist's own mind." I see, I hear, I perceive, I produce. Stevenson that summer, sitting idly under the madroñas in the shadow of the forge, was storing the treasure house of his mind.

He went to that treasure house for help with later writing, drawing upon his memories of Silverado for description and incident. Nowhere is this more obvious than in *Treasure Island*, where not only the Monterey Peninsula but the Mount Saint Helena country furnished setting after setting. *Treasure Island* is associated in many particulars with *The Silverado Squatters*, and even the wording of descriptions in the two books is sometimes the same. The tall pines "out-topping" all the other trees of the island were the tall pines Stevenson had seen when driving up Mount Saint Helena with old Friedberg. Again, "The hills ran up clear above the vegetation in spires of naked rock." That was Cathedral Rock to the east of Mount Saint Helena. And anyone seeing the great mountain from the lower end of the valley, so as to get the perspective, would realize the aptness of this description, applied to Spy-glass Hill: "All were strangely shaped, and the Spy-glass, which was by three or four hundred feet the tallest on the island, was likewise the strangest in configuration, running up sheer from almost every side, and then suddenly cut off at the top like a pedestal to put a statue on." Napa people locate Mount Saint Helena by this appearance of being cut off square at the top, as though the upper third had been eliminated.

The vegetation of *Treasure Island* was the vegetation of Mount Saint Helena—"contorted trees, not unlike the oak," "heavy-scented broom and many flowering shrubs," "thickets of green nutmeg trees," foliage of "poisonous brightness," the poison oak of Silverado, and the "broad shadow of the pines." The fresh spicy air, the sheer sunlight, the sliding gravel, the chirp of insects, even the rattlesnakes of Silverado are here! A comparison of the last chapter of *The Silverado Squatters* and the descriptive passages of *Treasure Island* would bring out many more similarities.

Nor was this the only tale that drew upon the Mount Saint Helena treasure house. The opening sentence of *Olalla* gave the setting not only of that story, but of Stevenson's going to Calistoga. "Now," said the doctor, "my part is done, and, I may say, with some vanity, well done. It remains only to get you out of this cold and poisonous city, and to give you two months of pure air and an easy conscience." The patient was sent to the mountains, "wild and rocky, partially covered with rough woods." And, again repeating phrases from *The Silverado Squatters*, Stevenson's "Journey with the Children of Israel" was transposed to Spain: "The sun shone; the wind rustled joyously; and we had advanced some miles, and the city had already shrunk into an inconsiderable knoll upon the plain behind us . . . ." Throughout the story, parts were borrowed from the California Coast Range.

The Wrecker drew largely upon San Francisco, of course, as did *The Bottle Imp* and *The Ebb Tide*. But there was in *The Wrecker* one reference to the country of *The Silverado Squatters*. Jim Pinkerton and Louden Dodd planned a trip to either the Napa Valley or Monterey. "It was to Calistoga that we went; there was some rumour of a Napa land-boom at the moment, the possibility of stir attracted Jim, and he informed me he would find a certain joy in looking on, much as Napoleon on St. Helena took a pleasure to read military works. The field of his ambition was quite closed; he was done with action; and looked forward to a ranch in a mountain dingle, a patch of corn, a pair of kine, a leisurely and contemplative age in the green shade of forests." But he didn't buy the ranch; "he was observed in consultation with the local editor, and owned he was in two minds about purchasing the press and paper." Scoop for the *Calistogian*!

Toils and Pleasures of the Summer

————◆◆◆►————

I must try to convey some notion of our
life, of how the days passed and what
pleasure we took in them, of what
there was to do and how
we set about doing it,
in our mountain
hermitage.

THERE WAS TOIL as well as fun in the gypsy life the royal family found so easy to adopt. Household tasks were laborious, but they were satisfying to primitive instincts —"the literal drawing of water, and the preparation of kindling, which it would be hyperbolical to call the hewing of wood"; the ancient rite of lighting the fire; the concoction of simple meals; the spreading of meadowsweet hay in the bunks. The Stevensons kept house as children do at play.

Louis, the King of Silverado, was the earliest riser. He brought in wood from Irvin Loveland's lazy woodpile and soon had the stove crackling in its corner. He set the coffee on to boil, cooked the breakfast cereal, and laid the table. Save for fetching an occasional pail of water, one of the pleasant tasks, this ended his housework for the day.

After the morning meal, the Queen "laboured singlehanded in the palace" while he had a sun bath in the azalea thicket above the well and did his setting-up exercises. This part of the day's program was fraught with some danger because of the rattlesnakes that loved the sun-warmed, ore-strewn hillside. The sun bather wrote of the rattlesnakes' nest with his tongue in his cheek, but the story was not pure fiction.

"Wherever we brushed among the bushes, our passage woke their angry buzz. One dwelt habitually in the wood-pile, and sometimes, when we came for firewood, thrust up his small head between two logs, and hissed at the intrusion. The rattle has a legendary credit; it is said to be awe-inspiring, and, once heard, to stamp itself forever in the memory. But the sound is not at all alarming; the hum of many insects, and the buzz of the wasp convince the ear of danger quite as readily. As a matter of fact, we lived for weeks in Silverado, coming and going, with rattles sprung on every side, and it never occurred to us to be afraid. I used to take sun-baths and do calisthenics in a certain pleasant nook among azalea and calycanthus, the rattles whizzing on every side like spinning-wheels, and the combined hiss or buzz rising louder and angrier at any sudden movement; but I was never in the least impressed, nor ever attacked."

After his calisthenics, this brave person settled himself in the shade of the madroñas that overhung the forge. Now he was engaged in labors of the mind. On some days there were letters he must write to family and friends abroad. On other days there were proof sheets, lately arrived at the Calistoga post office from his literary adviser, Sidney Colvin, in London, which must be corrected and sent back. Or he must set down the words of a poem that had been going through his head during sleepless hours of the night. But for the most part he was busy with his notes for the new book that was to record these daily doings.

In mid-morning the twelve-year-old Crown Prince left off trundling a toy-size railway car once used for ore.

He had been shunting it to the edge of the chute and back again. Reluctantly now he came for morning lessons in Latin and geometry, an ordeal that put his tutor to bed when it was over, but sent the boy bounding up the hill to the third floor room, where he was soon busy with his printing press.

While the lessons were in progress, sometimes the pretty Queen, a diminutive figure in a cotton frock of her own making, would swing open the mended door of the battered palace, and bring out her sewing or her sketching. All her life the Queen had liked gypsying; and here in this perfect summer climate, with the bright sunshine, the cool breezes, and the lack of rain, the tented heavens alone would have offered sufficient shelter for her family. Now that cleanliness and coziness had performed their miracle, Sam Chapman's old bunkhouse was a palace indeed. Here was home. And the Queen who reigned there, easing the inconveniences for the others, was a happy woman.

Upon her shoulders, it was true, the heaviest responsibilities had fallen, for her "dear boy" was still very much the invalid and required careful, tactful nursing. "I do try to take care of him," she had written his mother in one of her wistful letters from the mountain. And he was getting well! What more could she ask, this wife who had thought him dying when she married him?

Soon after lunch—on some days, before—her invalid was off on his walk to the Toll House, his dog at his heels. The Clear Lake stage left the Magnolia Hotel in Calistoga around noon, and Louis enjoyed the excitement of its arrival at the inn. If he was late, he hurried down by way of the short cut past his treasure grotto. But if there was time for a leisurely stroll, he took the longer trail that started at the grotto, made a half-circle to leftward, and finally plunged steeply downward, coming out, like the shorter path, behind the Toll House.

Along the way he had many a lesson in the flora and fauna of the mountain. Azaleas bloomed in damp shade. Calycanthus bushes spread their slender dark green branches, just beginning to push forth heavily scented blossoms of deep maroon. Mountain lilac tinted open slopes with a delicate mauve. Dogwood, hound's tongue, Indian paintbrush, Johnny-jump-up, and down among the grasses the last of spring's small delicate flowerlets —these were blooming at the season when Stevenson knew and loved the mountain.

Some of the trees were new to him. The nutmeg had lacy branches very like the redwood, and a fruit the size of a small plum with a spicy kernel at its core. The juiceless narrow leaves of the sweet bay, which the natives called "California laurel," had a pleasant aroma, as did the several conifers. There was the madroña with its orange bark; the manzanita with a twisted trunk the color of cinnabar. The maple, the buckeye, the live oak, and other varieties of oak that reminded him of England —all were there, with chaparral and chamiso brush making a thorny thicket on dry hillsides.

About midway of the trail, the stroller made a steep ascent, scrambling over rubble. The mountain here was bare of vegetation, the soil being covered by lava resembling a spongy dough grown hard. Here, too, were the balanced rocks which seemed to him poised for a sudden crashing plunge.

At this season not many birds were singing, and it took a close eye to detect their little forms among the shrubbery. He made note also of the kangaroo rat, a great curiosity to him. In the wild regions above there were grizzlies and cinnamon bears, mountain lions and wildcats, foxes and coyotes. But these creatures, chiefly nocturnal and always shy, never disturbed his wanderings. Occasionally a deer flashed past, or stood with innocent eyes observing him.

He half-slid down the last steep bit of path. Through the kitchen door of the inn he could see Mrs. Corwin, the landlord's wife, Mrs. Rankin, the cook, and the Chinese boy who assisted them. In the bar was Mr. Hoddy, who sometimes loaned him books or borrowed books from him. Corwin and Jennings dozed on the veranda; Hetty Prior, the schoolma'am, dozed with her mother and her lady friends in the parlor.

The summer term for the mountain children had opened on the seventeenth of May. Hetty, who boarded at the Toll House, had come from Red Bluff when her brother Alfred, who worked at the Great Western Mine, secured for her the Silverado school. Now every morning she walked down the toll road to the little brown "shanty" that had been moved from Silverado Flat to house the school children.

The inn to Louis Stevenson was a "kind of small Davos," a health resort inhabited by consumptives like himself, a suitable place "for a wasted life to doze away in." But the drowsy atmosphere he found upon his arrival gave way to hurry and expectancy when the two stages, one going north, the other south, swept up the road from opposite directions and halted at the toll bar, each spilling passengers, mail, and express.

"Huge concerns they were, well horsed and loaded, the men in their shirt sleeves, the women swathed in veils, the long whip cracking like a pistol; and as they charged upon that slumbering hostelry, each shepherding a dust storm, the dead place blossomed into life and talk and clatter. This the Toll House?—with its city throng, its jostling shoulders, its infinity of instant business in the bar? The mind would not receive it! The heartfelt bustle of that hour is hardly credible; the thrill of the great shower of letters from the post-bag, the childish hope and interest with which one gazed in all these strangers' eyes."

Charley Lawley, when he lived on the mountain, liked to tell about his meetings with R. L. S. at mail time.

"Stevenson used to sit here in front of the Toll House," he said. "Every day at stage time he'd come for the mail, taking the steep path through the woods. A crowd would gather here when the stages came in, and there was lots of noise and talking. He didn't mix much. He was always eager for his mail, and he got more, let me tell you, than all the rest of us put together! He'd open his letters, sitting out here in the sun, and then usually he'd write for awhile in his notebook. Sometimes he'd watch the croquet game, but I never saw him play.

"He used to talk with me sometimes, mostly about the scenery or the Hanson family that was neighbors to him at Silverado. The rest of us men hereabouts was always talking about hunting and fishing; but he wasn't strong enough to hunt and fish, so I couldn't talk with him about that. Sometimes I wished that we had more in common.

"The people at the Toll House were never in awe of him. We didn't know that he was anything out of the ordinary. He was a quiet man who minded his own business. All we knew about him was that he was living on the mountain for his health."

Occasionally, when Corwin, the landlord, wasn't dozing, the quiet health seeker engaged him in what he frankly called gossip. Here was one man who could satisfy to some slight degree his perennial interest in the ghost towns of the region. Corwin had told him about the quicksilver excitement that preceded Silverado. When he had arrived in Napa County twenty years before, there was a city of tents called Jonestown, with a population of two thousand, on the Lake County side of the mountain, while over toward the west was another encampment whose very name was lost.

"Both of these have perished, leaving not a stick and scarce a memory behind them. Tide after tide of hopeful miners have thus flowed and ebbed about the mountain, coming and going, now by lone prospectors, now with a rush."

A few of the more permanent towns were still in existence. High on a spur of the mountain, within walking distance of Silverado, was Oat Hill, named for one of the largest quicksilver mines in California, then employing fifty men. It was quite a place, having a company store, a post office, a schoolhouse, a church, and at that period no saloons, a condition that made it unique among mining towns. Not far from Oat Hill, but at a lower altitude, was the Phoenix mine and Phoenix town, boasting a library and reading room for the miners. Adjacent to the big Redington mine a few miles east of Oat Hill was Knoxville, then far from ghostly. Built on terraces cut into the hillside, it was notable for the company-owned buildings constructed of hewn stone in 1862. All three towns were well worth a visit.

"Last in order of time came Silverado, reared the big mill in the valley, founded the town which is now represented, monumentally, by Hanson's, pierced all these slaps and shafts and tunnels, and in turn declined and died away."

Following the quicksilver excitement, Corwin had seen the quest for silver and gold. "There was, he thought, scarce a rock on the whole mountain but what had been chipped at that time by the prospector's hammer." Some of his stories of Silverado were, however, not quite accurate, one especially to the effect that all the good ore had been taken from the "great upright seam" which Stevenson called the horizontal shaft.

Not all the gossip took place that summer at the Toll House. Decidedly on the pleasure side of the ledger were Stevenson's visits with Virgil and Dora Williams. Sometimes these were in his own outdoor parlor at the mine, more often on the veranda of the Williams' pleasant house among the pine trees, in a snug canyon to the west of Silverado.

Twice the Walker family from the Mansion House on the Spring Grounds came up the mountain to call, the little milkmaid climbing the perilous ropewalk plank to the second-floor room, where her former playmate sat surrounded by pillows in his upper berth, busy with his notes for *The Silverado Squatters.*

Several times Fanny went to call on friends of the Williams', the McDonald family, who had a ranch on the Geysers road in Knight's Valley; and once Louis went with her. The Scot, Frank McDonald, was a friend not only of Virgil Williams but of Fanny's first husband, and Louis himself had met him while at Calistoga and been asked to spend a day at his country home.

Many years later, Mrs. Maggie Turner, McDonald's daughter, gave a vivid account of this visit.

"I was just a youngster, but I can see Mr. Stevenson now, sitting on our front porch talking with my father and mother. How he squinted his black eyes and looked me up and down! I was one of those long-legged skinny little girls that would get self-conscious at the least little thing. When I came out on the porch, here was this stranger who immediately turned to see the Scotchman's little daughter. His looking at me so hard gave me the creeps: I remember to this day how I felt. I refused to talk to him or eat dinner with him. Can you beat that? Chicken dinner, too, for company!

"The grown folks' conversation was mostly about Scotland, as I recall. My father's home was Strathaven, Lanarkshire, and his aunt was housekeeper to the Duke of Hamilton. Mother was Scotch too and a famous cook. I remember our guests praised the dinner.

"After dinner Mrs. Stevenson asked Mother if she might smoke, and I'll never forget how shocked we were; we'd never known a woman who smoked. She was strikingly unconventional in appearance—small and plump, with a dumpy figure, and wearing her hair short in a day when women didn't. I remember once she wore a black and white Mother Hubbard from San Francisco. She was a great talker and she often talked with my father about her first husband, and in a very nice way.

"My father knew Sam Osbourne very well, so we got his side of the divorce. Osbourne kept sending his wife money while she was in France, and finally stopped sending when she stayed on and on. He went to her there when the little boy died. It was our impression that it was Osbourne who got the divorce. However that may be, there was lots of talk afterward. Lloyd wasn't with her when she called on us, and I don't remember meeting any of her family.

"As to Stevenson—well, he was tall, dark, very sallow. Big eyes that never missed a thing. Stoop-shouldered, thin. He coughed a good bit, but he was gay and interesting company. He said in regard to his ill-health, 'I brought this on myself: I went the pace.'

"Since that day I've read all his books and everything about him I could get hold of. Most of the biographies make him out too much of a saint, which I think spoils them."

Stevenson would have been not shocked but amused at this last statement. The friends who knew him best protested when Balfour's official biography characterized him as, in Henley's words, a "seraph in chocolate." Later biographers followed Balfour's lead, suppressing, except for veiled references, all information concerning the youthful excesses that followed the overstrict, "darkly religious" childhood of the odd, reserved, spoiled little Louis; excesses for which he paid dearly in health but which never robbed him of his chivalry toward women. Stevenson himself was frank enough about his lack of preparation for the world of reality, and already at Sil-

verado he was laying down precepts for the wiser up-
bringing of his stepson.

At some time during the summer that stepson fell
ill of diphtheria. When Fanny contracted the disease
also, Louis, "sick to begin with," found a cottage in
Calistoga and had the two patients moved down the
mountain. The only physician in Calistoga that summer
was Dr. A. W. Scott, and it was probably he who at-
tended Lloyd and his mother.

At the time of their return to their crude squatters'
quarters, Louis tried to find a servant for Fanny, who
was too listless now to take to gypsying with any zest.
Most household servants at that time in California were
Chinese, and they planned to give their servant the third-
floor room where other Chinese once had slept. Kong
Sam Kee, their laundryman, was entrusted with the affair.
According to Corwin's census figures, there were thirty-
four Chinese in the Calistoga district. Surely among
them was one who would go to Silverado. Kong Sam
Kee did produce a boy on the evening of their departure,
but he "was wedded to his washhouses," and the Stevensons climbed servantless into the wagon that took them
home.

"Joe Strong, the painter," paid two visits to Silverado
that summer, and on the second was accompanied by his
wife, Fanny's daughter Isobel, and his aunt, Nellie
Sanchez. Isobel later wrote a pleasant description of the
weeks which she and Joe and Nellie shared with the
Stevensons in the tumbledown palace.

"We had our meals out-of-doors, and as there never
was a better cook than Fanny Stevenson, they were good
ones. She used the mouth of the old Silverado mine for
an ice chest and storeroom; here hung sides of venison,
pigeons, wild ducks and other game purchased from
friendly neighbors, and in the chill shadow were cans
of fresh milk brought up the mountain each morning.

STEVENSON COTTAGE, CALISTOGA

Photograph by Anne Roller Issler

WHERE THE CABIN STOOD IN 1880

Photograph by Anne Roller Issler

"Though my mother was an excellent nurse, she was not a fussy one. There was never any suggestion at all of Louis' being an invalid, and everybody shared in the good things she·prepared for him. About eleven o'clock in the morning and three in the afternoon we were all served with rum punch, frothy with cream and delicately topped with a sprinkle of cinnamon.

"In the evenings we sat around the campfire talking, but soon the chill that always came at night, even after the hottest day, drove us to our beds."

The editor of the *Calistogian* learned of this visit, but only one of the group had news value—Robert Louis Stevenson's stepson-in-law. The following item appeared in the issue of the paper for July 21, 1880. "Strong, a San Francisco artist, is spending some time this summer in the upper Napa Valley and about Mount Saint Helena. He will tarry a couple of weeks, we understand, in the vicinity of the Toll House, for the purpose of making sketches at certain points, which he will reproduce on canvas during the coming fall and winter."

Joe Strong made several sketches of the immediate vicinity of the mine, setting up his easel on the platform; and several of Louis and Fanny. One sketch showed them inside the palace, Louis writing up his diary in bed, Fanny sewing while keeping him company.

Not until the very end of July did the little party— the King, the Queen, the Crown Prince, and their three guests—leave the mountain. Then they all went down to San Francisco together, Louis and Fanny taking rooms in the same apartment house in which they had lived during their first few days as man and wife. This was the house at 7 Montgomery (Columbus) Avenue, where Joe and Isobel had their studio and living quarters.

All through the summer the letters from Thomas and Maggie Stevenson had been urging Louis to return to Scotland and bring his wife and stepson "home." Fanny had at last pronounced the invalid well enough for the journey, and in a letter mailed at Calistoga on July 16, had written Louis' mother, "I trust that in about two weeks we shall be able to start, and perhaps in less time than that." It took longer than they had expected to stow away their belongings in the boxes they had carefully saved. Louis hovered over his books; Fanny mended and washed and pressed and carefully packed their clothes. Of household effects there were few at Silverado, and those left in Oakland would have to be sold or given to relatives. But the little printing press went along to Edinburgh and later to Davos in the Alps.

The last morning arrived. The Hansons were there, of course, to see them off, Rufe silent and grave as ever; his wife in a fresh print dress and sunbonnet, with voluble farewells and a few tears; Irvin shouldering the heavy boxes as easily as he had shouldered them on the day of the squatters' arrival; the children open-mouthed with wonder. The luggage went down to Calistoga on Hanson's wagon; the squatters and their guests took the stage. A last wave of the hand, a last look back, and they had gone.

Hail and Farewell

Doomed to know not Winter, only Spring, a being
Trod the flowery April blithely for awhile,
Took his fill of music, joy of thought and seeing,
Came and stayed and went, nor ever ceased to smile.

AND SO Mount Saint Helena saw no more of the scribbler. But the people of Napa County have not forgotten
him. They have their own tradition of Stevenson, a com-
posite delineation of his character that has come down
from the past like the sagas of old. Children and children's children have been brought up on *The Silverado
Squatters*. Tales and pageants and pilgrimages again
and again revive the story of his summer here. These
people love him ever, as a friend.

They remember, first of all, his very human self. The
people round about Calistoga were glad when the "seraph
in chocolate" fell off the pedestal so carefully built up
by his wife and the family biographer whose work she
superintended. It was the "true Stevenson" they had remembered, a man of both strength and weakness. His
foibles were less shocking to the sons of the forty-niners
than they had been to Calvinistic Edinburgh. In this
frontier community, cosmopolitan and realistic, decent
and respectable, but without blue laws in retrospect or
prospect, men's mistakes and their consequences were
less in need of whitewashing than in Victorian society.
Men did not condone each other's sins, but they assumed

their existence. Calistoga, and his neighbors on the mountain, accepted Stevenson as a man, not a seraph.

These neighbors remembered the traits he shared with the pioneers—especially his courage in the face of almost insurmountable obstacles, the gay heart that belied the frailty of his hold on life, the strong spirit's refusal to be bound by the body's weakness. Scorning pity as did the hardy sons of the West, Stevenson was above all a valiant fighter. True, he was seldom in pain, and his mind was often more buoyant and eager when he was confined to bed. But those who knew him did not, for all that, naïvely discount the rebellion of his manhood against weakness and lassitude. The irksomeness of his constant fight for health he revealed in a letter to Sidney Colvin written from Samoa when his brief life was almost over.

"I have endured some two and forty years without public shame, and had a good time as I did it. If only I could secure a violent death, what a fine success! I wish to die in my boots; no more land of counterpane for me. To be drowned, to be shot, to be thrown from a horse— ay, to be hanged, sooner than to pass again through that slow dissolution." He did die literally with his boots on, but he never left the hateful land of counterpane far behind.

Said a Calistoga woman whose father, remembering Stevenson, had read *The Silverado Squatters* to her in her childhood, "He was not robust, he kept to himself, he lived within his mind. They called him queer. What a struggle there must have been between his eager mind and his frail body! It is so satisfying a thought that this brave spirit, creating beauty, has cheered so many frail and sick who have read his books."

He was human, he was brave, he took life as an adventure. Always there was romance. He must flee the sea fogs: well, then he would be King of Silverado! He

118

would make a tumbledown shack into a palace that any king would envy.

To the settlers of Napa Valley, themselves romantic adventurers, this was the greatest bond with their neighbor, the scribbler. This feeling for romance remains the strongest link in the invisible chain reaching back to Stevenson's summer here. There lingers in the country of *The Silverado Squatters* something more than cold, hard fact. The sunshine over hill and valley hints of gold and silver as it touches the rich earth of vineyard, orchard, and forest. The streets of Calistoga echo faintly to footsteps that have ceased. Mount Saint Helena is not just a mound of volcanic soil covered with rocks and trees. Here the unraveling of time makes a continuous pattern of past, present, and future—a pattern of the interwoven personalities of many sorts of persons.

Stevenson was interested in every sort, but he liked the plain and simple better than the more sophisticated. In the course of his adventure with life, he sought out ordinary, folksy people like Charley Evans and Jacob Schram and Rufe Hanson. He liked them with a warmly human feeling, and they liked him in return. This explains his popularity as a writer. The common people heard him gladly because he was so interested in them.

Thirty-one years after he left Silverado, the women's clubs of Napa County dedicated to Stevenson a monument on Mount Saint Helena, in gratitude for his love of their people. A slab of Scotch granite in the shape of an open book was set up where once had stood his palace, and on it was engraved the verse that heads this chapter.

This was not the first memorial to Stevenson in California. San Francisco already had one, and was soon to have another. Three years after his death the Stevenson Fellowship had dedicated another monument of granite in Portsmouth Square, this one carrying a message from the "Christmas Sermon," written shortly after R. L. S.

left California. Crowning the monument was a little bronze ship under full sail, symbol of a venturesome life.

Especially appropriate was the second San Francisco memorial, dedicated by the Children's Hospital in 1914, following an appeal by the newspapers. A fund was raised for the perpetual endowment of a hospital room whose gaily decorated walls would bring happiness to many a sick child in this city where Stevenson had come so close to death.

Then, in Monterey, two public-spirited women purchased an old adobe house, the French Hotel, later presenting it to the State of California. Here R. L. S. had lived before coming to San Francisco. The Literary Anniversary Club, with elaborate ceremony, placed a bronze plaque on this "Stevenson House" in 1932, and in 1949 it was dedicated as a state historic monument.

And now Napa County comes forward again, with what is to be the most elaborate memorial of all. Now that legal and financial difficulties have been disposed of, there will be a Robert Louis Stevenson State Park on Mount Saint Helena. Purchased with funds contributed by people all over the world, it will embrace several hundred acres of woodland, including the whole locale of *The Silverado Squatters*, as it related to the mountain. The monument that looks like a stone book will remain to mark the site of the house. The land will be left as nearly as possible as it was when Stevenson spent his honeymoon there. And no lumberman will ever destroy the forest that shelters the site of that once busy little mining town, Silverado.

BIBLIOGRAPHY

BOOKS

A. The *Collected Works of Robert Louis Stevenson*, with emphasis on the following:

Letters to Family and Friends, Sidney Colvin (ed.), New York: Charles Scribner's Sons, 1897.

Across the Plains, New York: Charles Scribner's Sons, 1897.

The Amateur Emigrant, New York: Charles Scribner's Sons, 1897.

The Old Pacific Capital, New York: Charles Scribner's Sons, 1897.

A Modern Cosmopolis, New York: Charles Scribner's Sons, 1897.

The Silverado Squatters, New York: Charles Scribner's Sons, 1897.

The Silverado Diary (fragment), New York: Charles Scribner's Sons, 1925.

Treasure Island, New York: Charles Scribner's Sons, 1897.

Olalla, New York: Charles Scribner's Sons, 1897.

The Wrecker, New York: Charles Scribner's Sons, 1897.

Underwoods, New York: Charles Scribner's Sons, 1897.

New Poems, London: Chatto & Windus, 1918.

B. Biography and Criticism:

BALFOUR, SIR GRAHAM, *The Life of Robert Louis Stevenson*, New York: Charles Scribner's Sons, 1901.

BERMANN, RICHARD ARNOLD, *Home from the Sea; Robert Louis Stevenson in Samoa*, Indianapolis and New York: The Bobbs-Merrill Company, 1939.

BLAND, HENRY MEAD, *Stevenson's California*, San Jose, Calif.: Pacific Short Story Club, 1924.

BROWN, GEORGE EDWARD, *A Book of R. L. S.*, New York: Charles Scribner's Sons, 1919.

CARRÈ, JEAN MARIE, *The Frail Warrior*, New York: Coward-McCann, Inc., 1930.

CHESTERTON, GILBERT KEITH, *Robert Louis Stevenson,* New York: Dodd, Mead & Company, Inc., 1928.

DAICHES, DAVID, *Robert Louis Stevenson; A Revaluation,* Norfolk, Conn.: New Directions, 1947.

DALGLISH, DORIS N., *Presbyterian Pirate,* London and New York: Oxford University Press, 1937.

DARK, SIDNEY, *Robert Louis Stevenson.* London: Hodder & Stoughton, Ltd., 1931.

EHRSAM, T. G., *Bibliographies of Twelve Victorian Authors,* New York: H. W. Wilson Company, 1936.

FIELD, ISOBEL, *This Life I've Loved,* New York: Longmans, Green & Company, 1931.

FISHER, ANNE BENSON, *No More a Stranger,* Stanford, Calif.: Stanford University Press, 1946.

HAMMERTON, JOHN ALEXANDER, *In the Track of R. L. Stevenson and Elsewhere in Old France,* New York: E. P. Dutton & Co., Inc., 1908.

HAMMERTON, JOHN ALEXANDER, *Stevensoniana,* New York: Mansfield, 1900; Edinburgh: John Grant, 1907 and 1910.

HARPER, HENRY (ed.), *Poems and Prose Pieces of Robert Louis Stevenson Hitherto Unpublished,* Boston: Bibliophile Society, 1921.

HELLMAN, GEORGE SIDNEY, *The True Stevenson; A Study in Clarification,* Boston: Little, Brown & Company, 1925.

HEYDRICK, B. A., *Types of the Essay,* New York: Charles Scribner's Sons, 1921.

HINSDALE, HARRIET, *Robert Louis Stevenson* (a play), Caldwell, Idaho: Caxton Printers, Ltd., 1947.

ISSLER, ANNE ROLLER, *Happier for His Presence; San Francisco and Robert Louis Stevenson,* Stanford, Calif.: Stanford University Press, 1949.

LOW, WILL H., *A Chronicle of Friendships,* New York: Charles Scribner's Sons, 1908.

MASSON, ROSALINE ORME, (ed.), *I Can Remember Robert Louis Stevenson,* Edinburgh and London: W. & R. Chambers, Ltd., 1922.

MASSON, ROSALINE ORME, *The Life of Robert Louis Stevenson,* Edinburgh and London: W. & R. Chambers, Ltd., 1923.

MOORS, H. J., *With Stevenson in Samoa,* Boston: Small, Maynard & Company, 1911.

OSBOURNE, KATHERINE DURHAM, *Robert Louis Steven-*

son in California, Chicago: A. C. McClurg & Company, 1911.

OSBOURNE, SAMUEL LLOYD, *An Intimate Portrait of R. L. S.*, New York: Charles Scribner's Sons, 1924.

RALEIGH, WALTER, *Robert Louis Stevenson*, London: Edward Arnold & Co., 1910.

SANCHEZ, NELLIE VAN DE GRIFT, *The Life of Mrs. Robert Louis Stevenson*, New York: Charles Scribner's Sons, 1920.

STEUART, JOHN ALEXANDER, *Robert Louis Stevenson; Man and Writer*, Boston: Little, Brown & Company, 1924.

STEUART, JOHN ALEXANDER, *The Cap of Youth*, Philadelphia: J. B. Lippincott Company, 1927.

SWINNERTON, FRANK, *R. L. Stevenson; A Critical Study*, New York: Doubleday, Doran & Company, Inc., 1923.

C. Local History—Napa County, California, in 1880:

ALTROCCHI, JULIA COOLEY, *The Old California Trail*, Caldwell, Idaho: Caxton Printers, Ltd., 1945.

BANCROFT, HUBERT HOWE, *History of California*, Vol. VII, San Francisco: A. L. Bancroft, 1882.

BARTLETT, WILLIAM C., *A Breeze from the Woods*, Oakland, Calif.: privately printed, 1880.

BARI, VALESKA, (ed.), *The Course of Empire; First-hand Accounts of California in the Days of the Gold Rush*, New York: Coward-McCann, Inc., 1931.

BRYANT, EDWIN, *What I Saw in California*, Santa Ana, Calif.: Fine Arts Press, 1936.

BRIGGS, L. VERNON, *California and the West*, San Francisco: privately printed, 1881.

CAMP, WILLIAM MARTIN, *San Francisco; Port of Gold*, New York: Doubleday & Company, Inc., 1947.

CLELAND, ROBERT GLASS, *From Wilderness to Empire; A History of California, 1542–1900*, New York: The Macmillan Company, 1944.

COOK, S. F., *The Conflict Between the California Indians and White Civilization*, Berkeley and Los Angeles: University of California Press, 1943.

DANE, G. EZRA, *Ghost Town*, New York: Alfred A. Knopf, Inc., 1941.

DARMS, H., *Portfolio and Directory of Napa City*, Napa, Calif.: H. A. Darms, 1908.

123

DeVoto, Bernard, *The Year of Decision: 1846,* Boston: Little, Brown & Company, 1943.

Doxey, William, *California Tourist Guide,* San Francisco: Doxey and Company, 1881.

Federal Writers' Project, *California; A Guide to the Golden State,* American Guide Series, New York: Hastings House, 1939.

Gift, George W., *Something About California: Napa County, Its Agriculture, Vineyards, Health, and Population,* Napa, Calif.: Reporter Book Press, 1876.

Gregory, Thomas Jefferson, *History of Solano and Napa Counties,* Los Angeles: Historic Record Company, 1912.

Gunn, Harry Lawrence, *History of Napa County, California,* Chicago: J. S. Clarke Publishing Company, 1926.

Harlan, Jacob Wright, *California from '46 to '88,* San Francisco: A. L. Bancroft, 1888.

Harlow, Alvin F., *Old Waybills,* New York and London: D. Appleton-Century Company, Inc., 1934.

History of Napa and Lake Counties, San Francisco: Slocum & Bowan, 1881.

Hoover, Mildred Brooke, *Historic Spots in California,* Stanford, Calif.: Stanford University Press, 1937.

Illustrations of Napa County, California; with Historical Sketch, Oakland, Calif.: Smith & Elliott, 1878.

Jackson, Joseph Henry, *Anybody's Gold,* D. Appleton-Century Company, Inc., 1941.

Jones, Idwal, *The Vineyard* (a novel), New York: Duell, Sloane & Pearce, Inc., 1942.

Kroeber, A. L., *Elements of Culture in Native California,* Berkeley: University of California Press, 1922.

Menefee, Campbell Augustus, *Sketchbook of Napa, Sonoma, Lake and Mendocino Counties,* Napa, Calif.: Reporter Publishing House, 1873.

Memorial and Biographical History of Northern California, Chicago: The Lewis Publishing Company, 1891.

McKenney's District Directory of Napa County, California, 1878–79.

McKittrick, Myrtle, *Vallejo, Son of California,* Portland, Ore.: Binford and Mort, 1944.

Murphy, Celeste, *The People of the Pueblo,* Sonoma, Calif.: W. L. and C. G. Murphy, 1937.

Napa Ladies Seminary Catalogs, 1878–80.

Paulson, L. L., *Handbook and Directory of Napa County*, San Francisco: Francis & Valentine, 1874.

Peattie, Roderick (ed.), *The Pacific Coast Ranges*, "Farm, Rock and Vine Folk," by Idwal Jones, New York: The Vanguard Press, 1946.

Revere, Joseph Warren, *A Tour of Duty in California*, New York and Boston: J. H. Francis, 1849.

Scott, Reva, *Samuel Brannan and the Golden Fleece*, New York: The Macmillan Company, 1946.

Wallace, W. F., *History of Napa County*, Oakland, Calif.: Enquirer Press, 1901.

ARTICLES IN MAGAZINES AND JOURNALS

"Robert Louis Stevenson, His Work and Personality," *Bookman* (extra number), London: Hodder & Stoughton, Ltd., 1913.

Bidwell, John, "Life in California Before the Discovery of Gold," *Century* (December 1890).

French, Harold, "Silverado," *Overland* (September 1906).

Issler, Anne Roller, "Quicksilver Mines of Northern California," *The Mining Journal* (April 15, 1942).

Marsh, O. C., "The Petrified Forest," *American Journal of Science and Arts*, Vol. I (January–June 1871).

"The Petrified Forest," *Proceedings, California Academy of Sciences*, Vol. XI, No. 19, 1922.

Ross, J. Edgar, "Silverado Today," *Overland* (March 1909).

Sessions, John, "Observations in California During 1855," *Quarterly, Society of California Pioneers*, Vol. V, No. 1 (March 1928).

Stevenson, Robert Louis, "My First Book, 'Treasure Island,' " *McClure's* (September 1894).

Stevenson, Robert Louis, "The Silverado Squatters" (earliest version), *Century* (November and December, 1883).

NEWSPAPERS

Brooklyn Home Journal (East Oakland), February 3, 1872, to December 14, 1872.

Calistoga Tribune, June 15, 1871, to December 31, 1873.

Calistoga Free Press, May 9, 1874, to October 16, 1875.

Independent Calistogian, December 26, 1877, to August 11, 1880.

Napa Register (weekly), January 1, 1874, to December 31, 1875.
Napa Register (daily), December 1, 1879, to August 2, 1880.
Saint Helena Star, October 9, 1874, to August 13, 1880.
Saint Helena Star (Grand Army Edition), July 16, 1886.

UNPUBLISHED MANUSCRIPTS

"Bear Flag Papers," Bancroft Library, University of California.

DAVIS, DEE T., "Stories of Napa County," research study compiled for Napa Junior College, Napa, Calif., 1942.

HANRAHAN, VIRGINIA, "Napa County History, 1823–1948," research study compiled for Napa Chamber of Commerce, Napa, Calif., 1949.

HUTCHINSON, FRED C., "Sam Chapman," research study, Berkeley, Calif., 1949.

ISSLER, ANNE ROLLER, "Silverado, 1874," research study compiled for Napa County Historical Society, Napa, Calif., 1948.

MOORE, FANNY CAROLINE, "Robert Louis Stevenson's First Visit to America," Master's thesis, Stanford University, Stanford, Calif., 1914.

OSBOURNE, LLOYD, "Reminiscences of R. L. S." (essay), December 20, 1922. Collection of Mrs. Ethel Osbourne, Gilroy, Calif.

OWEN, FRANK, "Early Days at Zem Zem," research study compiled for Napa County Historical Society, Napa, Calif., 1948.

"Pioneer Sketches," Bancroft Library, University of California, Berkeley, Calif.

PETER, HUBERT J., "The Crossroads of Nations," text for the Napa County Centennial Pageant, 1948–49, produced by Napa Junior College, Napa, Calif.

STEWART, GEORGE RIPPEY, "Stevenson in California. A Critical Study," Master's thesis, University of California, Berkeley, Calif., 1920.

TURNER, MAGGIE, "The Oak Knoll Ranch," research study compiled for Napa County Historical Society, Napa, Calif., 1948.

WILLIAMS, DORA NORTON, "Recollections of Robert Louis Stevenson," paper read before the Century Club of San Francisco, November 13, 1897. Original handwritten manuscript in Heron Collection, San Francisco, Calif.

UNPUBLISHED LETTERS

OSBOURNE, FANNY M. (later Mrs. Robert Louis Stevenson), Some thirty-five letters to her friend Timothy Rearden, 1874–81. Most are of the French period prior to and during Stevenson's courtship. Property of Mrs. Anna Rearden Beck, Berkeley, Calif.

REARDEN, TIMOTHY, Letter to his family, June 18, 1880, concerning Stevenson's marriage. Property of Mrs. Anna Rearden Beck, Berkeley, Calif.

STEVENSON, ROBERT LOUIS, Letter to Timothy Rearden concerning his wife's Oakland property, Barbizon, France, undated, probably 1881. Property of Mrs. Anna Rearden Beck, Berkeley, Calif.

INDEX

Frisbie House, 4, 9, 13; barroom in, 5, 6
Frisby House, *see* Frisbie House

Gardner, Charles A., 100
Garnet Street (Silverado), 81
Germany, 48, 50, 51
Geysers, 14, 20, 25, 31, 32, 33, 39, 55
Geysers Hotel, 31
Geysers road, *see* Foss toll road
Ghost towns, 29, 54, 55, 110, 111
Glasgow, Scotland, 42, 95
Gold (in Napa County), 62, 76, 79, 87, 111, 119; *see also* Calistoga Gold and Silver Mine, Gold Rush
Gold Rush, 37, 47, 51, 76, 79, 87
Gold Street (Silverado), 81, 82
Golden Gate, 7
Great Western Mine, 109
Greenock, Scotland, 42, 46, 47
Grez, France, 22, 23, 102
Grindoff (in *The Miller and His Men*), 35
Grist mill, *see* Bale Mill
Guèle, *see* Guile family
Guile family, 38, 64, 65

Hamilton, Duke of, 112
Hansen, *see* Hanson
Hansome, *see* Hanson
Hanson, Bill, 87
Hanson, Mary Jane (Mrs. Rufe), 38, 63, 85, 86, 92, 116; discussed by Stevenson, Lucy Ann Cole, and Charley Lawley, 91
Hanson, Nancy, 87
Hanson, Rufe, 36, 38, 57, 62, 68, 70, 72, 74, 77, 84, 110, 111, 116, 119; as claim-jumper, 85–87; discussed by Charley Lawley, 90, 91, 93; discussed by Mollie Patten, 87, 89; discussed by Stevenson, 89–90; as Gold Rush pioneer, 87; likened to Stevenson, 93
Haraszthy, Count Ágoston, 52; wine experiments of, 52–53
Headley, Franklin, 83
Healdsburg, California, 31
Hearsts, the, 28
"Hebrew tyrant," *see* Friedberg, Morris
Henley, William Ernest, 99

"Highwaymen," *see* Stage robbers
Hoddy, G. P., 84, 109; discussed by Stevenson, Mollie Patten, and Calistoga editor, 60–61
Hog's Back (mountain), 31
"Horizontal shaft," *see* Calistoga Gold and Silver Mine, shafts of
Horn, the, *see* Cape Horn
Horses, the Stevensons', *see* Clavel, Star
Hot Springs Hotel and Grounds, 3, 11, 12, 39, 45, 54, 64, 88, 112; bath-houses at, 20, 21, 28; cottages at, 20, 26, 27, 28; description of, by Stevenson, 27; drawings of, discussed, 27; history and description of, 25–26; as "oven place" of Indians, 17; rates at, 28; skating pavilion at, 26; as temporary home of Stevenson, 20, 21, 25, 28
Hotel Chapman, *see* Stevenson's bunkhouse, Silverado
Hudson Bay, 18
Hyères, France, 98

I Can Remember Robert Louis Stevenson, 67
"In Memoriam, F. A. S.," x; quoted (in chapter heading), 117
"In the States," 97
Independent Calistogian, see Calistogian
Indiana, 22, 61
Indians, 15, 52, 90; Stevenson's regard for, 17–18
"Indifference," 95
Industrial revolution, 56
Inland Voyage, An, 37, 97, 98
Irish family (South Vallejo), 8
"It is not yours, O Mother, to complain," 97
Italy, 51

Japanese tea garden (Brannan's), 26
Jennings, Frank, 60, 61, 109
Jennings, John D., 61
Johnson, Major George W., 24, 27, 45
Johnson, Mrs. G. W., 45
"Jones, the Welsh blacksmith," 37
Jonestown, California, 110
Juarez, Cayetano, 16

135

James Stevenson Publisher
California History books:

Historical and Descriptive Sketchbook of Napa, Sonoma
Lake and Mendocino, 1873
ISBN 1-885852-00-2

Memoirs of the Vallejos
ISBN 1-885852-02-9

William B. Ide, President of California
ISBN 1-885852-01-0

History of Solano County, 1879
ISBN 1-885852-03-7

The Capital That Couldn't Stay Put,
The Complete Book of California's Capitols
ISBN 1-885852-04-5

Sam Brannan, Builder of San Francisco
ISBN 1-885852-05-3

also available :
History of Alameda County, 1883
(1969 reprint by Holmes Book Company)
ISBN 1-885852-06-1

See title page to contact James Stevenson Publisher

World Wide Web site at:
http://www.community.net/~stevensn/publish.html